Father Joseph Ch. ... ... pastoral approach and style, has provided parish ministers with an excellent resource in approaching delicate pastoral issues. Those who utilize his approach will not only be "walking with the Church" in its legal system, but will also be treating those who come for assistance from Church ministers with respect and encouragement.

> Rev. Kevin McKenna, JCD
> Pastor, St. Cecilia Church, Rochester, New York
> Former President, Canon Law Society of America

As one involved in many years of Pastoral Ministry, *Firm, But Kind and Gentle* says it all, a must read for everyone.

> Sister Maureen D'Onofrio, CSJ, Pastoral Associate
> Cathedral of the Immaculate Conception
> Syracuse, New York

Monsignor Joseph Champlin is the undisputed dean of Catholic pastors in this country. Every word he writes has "pastor" written all over it. There isn't anyone in church ministry, lay or ordained, who would not profit from reading this fine book.

> Rev. Michael G. Ryan
> Pastor, St. James Cathedral, Seattle

Father Champlin spells out the need for firmness in presenting the truths of faith and the no less pressing need in applying these truths. This book provides guidance and encouragement not only for those in ministry, but for all Christian believers striving to live out their faith.

> Rev. John Eudes Bamberger, OCSO, Retired Abbot
> The Abbey of the Genesee, Piffard, New York

Firm, But Kind and Gentle is a treasure for anyone in ministry in the Catholic Church. Fr. Champlin's deep wisdom from decades of parish experience distills for us the "spirit of the law" rather than "the letter."

It is an invaluable guide for complex pastoral issues, and an inspiring reminder of the compatibility of fidelity and compassion.

Patricia Livingston, speaker, author of *Let in the Light, Facing the Hard Stuff with Hope* (Ave Maria Press).

Father Champlin has given us an eminently pastoral tool to aid in applying official church norms to pastoral circumstances. By presenting familiar scenarios and then leading toward a pastoral response, Father Champlin avoids quick fix answers in favor of teaching us how to be "firm, but kind and gentle." This book will be valuable for those who are first entering into pastoral ministry as well as those who have years of experience but are open to a review of their pastoral style. *Firm, But Kind and Gentle* is like having your own personal mentor in a book.

Fr. Ron Lewinski, Pastor
St. Mary of the Annunciation, Mundelein, Illinois

Fr. Champlin has written a book from his heart and incorporated the Solomon wisdom which comes from years of pastoral ministry. He shares many pastoral stories of decisions that were made with the goal of "...bringing all of us to a quiet harbor."

Barbara Smith, Director of Catechetics and Initiation
Diocese of Portland, Maine

FIRM, BUT KIND AND GENTLE

FIRM, BUT KIND AND GENTLE
A Practical Handbook for Pastoral Ministry

Father Joseph M. Champlin

ST PAULS

Library of Congress Cataloging-in-Publication Data

Champlin, Joseph M.
   Firm, but kind and gentle : a practical handbook for pastoral ministry / by Joseph
M. Champlin.
        p. cm.
   Includes bibliographical references.
   ISBN 13: 978-0-8189-1254-2
   ISBN 10: 0-8189-1254-5
   1. Pastoral theology—Catholic Church.   I. Title.

BX1913.C43 2007
253—dc22

                                         2007014721

Imprimatur:
✠ Most Reverend Thomas J. Costello, DD
Vicar General, Diocese of Syracuse, New York
Feast of St. John Vianney
August, 2006

Produced and designed in the United States of America by the
Fathers and Brothers of the Society of St. Paul,
2187 Victory Boulevard, Staten Island, New York 10314-6603
as part of their communications apostolate.

ISBN 13: 978-0-8189-1254-2
ISBN 10: 0-8189-1254-5

Printing Information:

Current Printing - first digit   1   2   3   4   5   6   7   8   9   10

Year of Current Printing - first year shown

2007   2008   2009   2010   2011   2012   2013   2014   2015   2016

DEDICATION

May Mary, the mother of the Church
bring us all to a quiet harbor

TABLE OF CONTENTS

INTRODUCTION

Pope Benedict XVI surprised people by his words and actions when he began serving as the Roman Catholic Church's chief shepherd.

Some judged that as Prefect of the Congregation for the Doctrine of the Faith he had issued icy condemnations of homosexual relations and had harshly silenced certain theologians. These persons expected more of the same when he became the Holy Father.

Pope Benedict, to the delight of many and the disappointment of others, has projected a quite opposite image.

The Tablet, an International Catholic Weekly, founded in 1840 and published in London, reported on three incidents which characterize this different approach.

A July 15, 2006 article entitled "The Softly, Softly Pope," describes a July visit to Spain for the Fifth World Meeting of Families, a country with the world's most liberal or extensive legislation about same sex marriage.

On the flight from Rome, he told reporters that he was not going to preach fire and brimstone, but rather would encourage the good things that were happening with families. He said, "Let's not start immediately with the negative."

Upon the Pope's return to Rome he continued in a positive tone, saying that the marriage covenant, when a man and a woman establish a permanent bond, "is a great good for humanity."

An August 19, 2006 *Tablet* piece contains an edited version of his conversation with four German broadcast journalists. The article, "The Power of Positive Thinking," includes this response by Pope Benedict:

"Christianity, Catholicism isn't a collection of prohibitions: It's a positive option. It's very important that we look at it again because this idea has almost completely disappeared today."

The Tablet, on September 2, 2006, published an editorial, "The New-Style Papacy," remarking that Pope Benedict has been stressing the virtues of leisure and the dangers of activism. The Holy Father quoted and made his own the words of St. Bernard of Clairvaux who said that "Much work often leads to hardness of heart."

This book seeks to exemplify a similar soft and positive dimension of the Catholic Church, even while honestly acknowledging certain aspects or actions that seem hard and harsh to some.

It is, in certain ways, a sequel to my *The Marginal Catholic: Challenge Don't Crush* which originally appeared nearly two decades ago and, in updated form, ten years later.[1]

The book's central theme is this: Official Catholic documents and directives which seek to be faithful to Christ's teachings and the Church's long traditions are also surprisingly flexible in their applications to specific pastoral situations.

While reflecting firmness and fidelity, they at the same time frequently mirror in their flexibility a kind and gentle spirit.

My book has been written especially for the clergy, priests and deacons, as well as for the increasing number of pastoral ministers who regularly encounter situations like those treated in

---

[1] Joseph M. Champlin, *The Marginal Catholic* (Staten Island, NY: Alba House, 2001).

this book. Readers will find here a reassurance and a challenge for both those who in practical circumstances incline to being firm or faithful and those who lean toward being gentle or flexible.

Father Joseph Champlin
Lent 2007

CHAPTER ONE

FAITHFUL, YET FLEXIBLE

When the late Terence Cardinal Cooke first met with his priests for the Archdiocese of New York he offered these words of pastoral guidance: "Be kind to our people."

Two decades later, a successor, Edward Cardinal Egan, interestingly gave almost identical advice to the clergy as he began his own ministry there. "Be kind to the people. Most of the negative communications which come to our office complain that a priest was unkind to them during some encounter."

Pope Benedict XVI, celebrating his first anniversary as the Holy Father, expressed this hope: That he would be a "firm and gentle shepherd" of Roman Catholics throughout the world.

The word "firm" in terms of the Church or Church leadership can have a very negative ring to it for some, perhaps many persons. They equate the word with "harsh and cruel, rigid and inflexible."

Here are several examples which many might judge to be "firm" actions in a negative sense:

➤ The dismissal of moralist Charles Curran as a Catholic theologian

➤ Requirement of an annulment before remarriage in the Church

➤ Refusal of baptism because the parents are not married, or not attending Mass, or not registered in the parish

➤ Rejection of a request for the Catholic funeral and burial of one who died by suicide

➤ Designation of homosexual acts as "intrinsically disordered."[1]

➤ Forbidding Catholic agencies to process adoption of children by partners in a same sex relationship

➤ Current preoccupation with the translation of liturgical texts when seemingly much more critical issues face the Church and the world

➤ Unwillingness to discuss the ordination of married men given the shortage of priests

➤ Reluctance to provide inclusive language in official worship texts

➤ Refusal to baptize infants adopted by same sex couples who attend Mass faithfully and promise to raise the child Catholic

➤ Turning away a couple who seek a marriage in the Church because they are cohabitating

➤ The Church's treatment of women

➤ Over-emphasis on money

➤ The sexual abuse scandals

➤ Non-response to requests for pastoral visits to the sick and dying

➤ Denying Holy Communion to the divorced and remarried

➤ Hurtful experiences in confession

➤ Abrupt, insensitive and "unkind" treatment by the clergy or pastoral ministers

---

[1] *Catechism of the Catholic Church* (New York: Doubleday, 1995), Article 2357.

Earthen Vessels

This list of painful experiences, while lengthy, is not exhaustive. People who have suffered through any or a few of them, however, quickly label such "firmness" as harsh and cruel, rigid and inflexible.

Some of these experiences of unkind treatment or confessional insensitivity, for example, can be traced simply to the human weakness of the clergy or pastoral ministers. Religious leaders obviously carry their treasures in earthen vessels or, in words of a contemporary scientist, "the truth of spiritual clean water is often placed in rusty containers."[2]

Unfortunate and regrettable as are those dark occurrences, we should not be surprised.

Jesus cautioned his three drowsy apostles in Gethsemane to pray because the "spirit is willing, but the flesh is weak" (Matthew 26:41).

Despite this warning and the fact that he was God's Son, miracle worker and supreme teacher, Christ's twelve apostles either betrayed, abandoned or denied him.

Catholics understand and grudgingly accept such frail humanness and the personal failings of leaders in education, government, and business. On the other hand, they generally feel very disillusioned or angered when hearing about or actually experiencing any of the unpleasant situations noted above within the Church.

Some such incidents have occurred because the local clergy or pastoral ministers were more strict and rigid than the official Church. Either lacking a complete knowledge of Church directives or possessing somewhat inflexible temperaments, they refused what the Church actually would permit.

---

[2] Francis S. Collins, *The Language of God* (New York: Free Press, 2006), p. 40.

Courageous Leaders

Others of these experiences could be attributed to leaders who conscientiously espouse and adhere to Christ's teachings and to the Church's traditions. Viewed from that perspective, "firm" and "firmness" might be seen in a more positive light.

Jesus displayed this type of firmness on many occasions. When, for example, in John 6, Christ gave his definitive teaching about the Eucharist, some listeners quarreled with him. Others complained, saying that it was a hard message and questioned whether anyone could accept it. However, the Lord did not back down or compromise his words. As a result, "many of his disciples returned to their former way of life and no longer accompanied him." Jesus did not plead with or pursue those objectors, but turned to the Twelve and asked, "Do you also want to leave?" Peter responded: "To whom shall we go? You have the words of eternal life" (John 6:66-69).

Visionary persons need to exercise this noble firmness when they meet sometimes fierce opposition in their pursuit of desirable goals. In his classic *Profiles in Courage*, John F. Kennedy sketched the lives of certain political leaders in our nation who maintained what they judged to be right and correct, although unpopular positions, even when doing so meant the possible end of their careers.

Parents of adolescents likewise face the often daunting task of being firm, but gentle with their teenage children when the prevailing climate seems overly permissive. A very successful veteran educator is known for his strict disciplinary rules in the classroom and during extra curricular activities. He contends that too many parents today seek to be friends to their children instead of guides and guardians. As a consequence, this instructor maintains too many dads and moms countenance, if not sponsor, underage drinking parties and allow participation in unchaperoned events or permit their offspring to dress inappropriately.

Parents who wish to be firm and oppose such laxity will no doubt hear complaints and objections from their children: "Everyone is doing it; their parents don't object; why are you so strict?" Praiseworthy firmness is not easy.

An Overview

The thrust of this book is not to clarify all of the difficult situations which we have summarized earlier, or even any of them. Nevertheless, in explaining or exemplifying its central theme — fidelity and flexibility — we will touch upon some of those experiences. For example, Chapter 7 will discuss the challenge when same sex parents seek the baptism of their adopted child and Chapter 8 will discuss annulments in the Catholic Church.

A note of clarification and caution for the reader: The chapters which follow will seek to demonstrate how official Church directives and documents are faithful in upholding Christ's words and our cherished traditions, yet also are remarkably flexible in their application to practical circumstances.

The initial chapters provide general comments to assist the clergy and pastoral ministers as they encounter complex particular situations. Thus, those sections offer a realistic vision of the parish or faith community, a correct understanding of Church law, the personal and ongoing nature of one's faith journey, and biblical insights from the Old and New Testament on how best to proceed pastorally.

The final five chapters examine specific areas to illustrate the faithful, yet flexible approach.

These focus mainly on baptism, marriage and funerals, key occasions which present opportunities for being firm, but kind and gentle.

Each chapter treats several specific, but quite different concerns related to the topic of that chapter. For example, "Burying the Dead" examines Words of Remembrance, Cremation, Intercommunion and Music. The reader, therefore, must leap mentally from one distinct issue to another to another and still another — all very different matters, but nevertheless each related to the theme of funerals or burying the dead.

This volume identifies many real and actual challenges which frequently occur in the life of the clergy and pastoral ministers. But they do not exhaust all the issues to be faced. This is not a massive manual concerning every pastoral problem and detailing the precise proper solution. Still, it contains in the beginning general principles which apply to all situations. Moreover, the later chapters contain, as described by a retired priest reviewer of this manuscript, "a wonderful cornucopia of practical suggestions for the book's target audience."

Challenge, Don't Crush

A final word about *fidelity and firmness*

The subtitle of my earlier book on this subject is "Challenge, Don't Crush." For example, carefully following biblical precepts, faithfully walking in Jesus' footsteps, and precisely observing Church teachings will be a real challenge. In fact, some would maintain that it is impossible to do so perfectly.

That impossibility, however, can be a stepping stone to spiritual growth, recognizing in our weaknesses the absolute need for God's grace and mercy.

Consider, as an illustration, Christ's injunction about perfect love. Jesus summons us to care about our neighbor as ourselves, to practice, on a daily basis and on every occasion, self-giving instead of self-seeking. Is anyone capable of achieving that goal?

Do we have an example of a single person who has done that to perfection? Even canonized saints failed at times.

Moreover, those committed to living out these ideals in today's world must also and often struggle in our contemporary society against trends which runs contrary to those principles. They encounter a culture of death as opposed to a culture of life, sexual permissiveness instead of Christian chastity, and a constant consumer oriented advertising campaign which seeks to transform our wants into our needs.

It is for the clergy and pastoral ministers during those many personal exchanges, especially in connection with requests for sacramental services, to challenge the petitioners with these spiritual goals. In a positive and informed way, their firm and faithful task is to encourage people to grow, to stretch a bit, to strive for the ideal.

A final word about *flexibility and kindness*

The second part of that subtitle is "Don't Crush."

This exhortation mirrors the description of the promised Messiah in Isaiah's prophecy and the realization of that prediction in Jesus. The Savior was to come, not shouting or crying out, but very careful not to break the bruised reed or snuff out the smoldering wick.

The Church in its official directives seeks to uphold the ideal — the challenge aspect — but always to recognize the limitations and weaknesses of its members — the don't crush dimension.

Chapter 3 on "Life and Laws" will demonstrate how the Church's legal system is amazingly flexible, offering numerous methods for adapting to particular circumstances.

In the latter portion of this book, the reader will also discover how the official directives for specific sacramental rites provide further explicit guidelines making adaptation to individual situations not only permissible, but desirable.

The complex and delicate task for clergy and pastoral ministers is to challenge with fidelity and firmness, while, at the same time, to extend fidelity and kindness, thus not crushing those marginal persons who approach them for sacramental services.

An Example

Four documents — the *Rite of Baptism for Children*, a 1980 *Instruction on Infant Baptism*, the 1983 *Code of Canon Law* and the 1994 *Catechism of the Catholic Church* — all stress that this sacrament is necessary for salvation and, moreover, that there must be a well-founded hope (*spes fundata*) that the baptized child will receive an authentic education in the faith and Christian life. These official texts also contain numerous directives for the proper celebration of the sacrament, rules which address such specific issues as time and place of baptism, requirements for sponsors, and the preparation of parents.

The documentation is clearly faithful to Christ's teaching, even with a certain firmness. But these regulations also include a flexibility, a kind and gentle approach to actual circumstances. A few illustrations of that flexible dimension:

➤ The 1980 Vatican *Instruction on Infant Baptism* includes a section which examines the issue of responding to "Families with little faith or non-Christian families." It describes the situation in these words:

It sometimes happens that pastors are approached by parents who have little faith and practice their religion only occasionally, or even by non-Christian parents who request baptism for their children for reasons that deserve consideration (No. 30).

The Instruction then provides guidelines for determining the appropriateness of baptizing such children.

> ➤ The *Code of Canon Law* includes these two regulations sensitively providing exceptions to the general norms:
>   i. Sponsors must be 16 unless "it seems to the pastor or minister that an exception is to be made for a just cause" (Canon 873).
>   ii. A baptized non-Catholic may serve as a witness to baptism providing there is also a Catholic sponsor (Canon 874:2).

The chapters which follow hopefully will help those serving and being served in pastoral situations realize that the official Catholic Church while firm and faithful, is also more flexible, gentle and kind than they may have thought.

CHAPTER TWO

ELITIST OR INCLUSIVE

What is your vision of the Church?
Is it a community of strong believers, generous givers and regular Mass goers?

Or

Is it a mix of daily Mass goers, every-Sunday worshipers, occasional participants at the weekly Eucharist, Christmas and Easter only attendees, as well as some we often termed "hatched, matched and dispatched" Catholics, present in church solely for their own baptisms, weddings and funerals?

Our vision of the Church, especially on the parish level, as elitist (the former) or inclusive (the latter), will greatly influence the approach we take to pastoral matters. This chapter will explore that crucial issue.

The Past Half-Century

When Catholic Bishops throughout the world gathered in Rome from 1961-1965 for the Second Vatican Council, the first document they discussed and approved was the *Constitution on the Sacred Liturgy*. This document contains rich theological and spiritual reflections on the liturgy, but also called for a major reform in the Church's worship rituals. The changes would include opening the scriptures more widely for the people, for example, or introducing the use of vernacular languages in the liturgy. That renewal process required about ten years to complete and implement.

Roman Catholic worship, consequently, since the early 1970's has been celebrated according to these new rites. Americans have generally been quite positive in their response to these restored rituals, particularly the expanded Lectionary of biblical readings, and the provision affording engaged couples the opportunity to participate in preparing their nuptial services as well as involving bereaved families in planning details of funeral liturgies.

However, an intense and vocal minority has expressed displeasure with some, and even all of the liturgical changes.

Moreover, these critics also objected to many subsequent liturgical additions or adaptations on the local level which they claim exceeded the reformed rules and violated correct worship practices.

Some of their complaints clearly were given a sympathetic hearing by Roman authorities. As a result in recent years, the Church, in fact has taken a few, but major official steps to correct liturgical "abuses" that have developed.[1] Moreover, the principle for translating Latin texts of ritual books into vernacular languages has been shifted from "dynamic equivalence," operative since 1969, to a "literal translation."[2]

The content of authoritative ritual books published over the next decade will reflect these changes.

---

[1] "Instruction on the Eucharist," Congregation for Divine Worship and the Discipline of the Sacraments (Washington, DC: USCCB Publishing, 2004).

[2] "The Authentic Liturgy," (*Liturgiam Authenticam*), Congregation for Divine Worship and the Discipline of the Sacraments (Washington, DC: United States Conference of Catholic Bishops, 2001).

Acts of Faith

Three articles of the *Constitution on the Sacred Liturgy* have exerted a major impact upon current Roman Catholic life and worship.

Article 59 states that the sacraments are "sacraments of faith"; "they not only presuppose faith, but by words and objects they also nourish, strengthen and express it." The faithful "should easily understand the sacramental signs, and should eagerly frequent those sacraments...."

Article 7 teaches that "Christ is always present in his Church, especially in her liturgical celebrations."

Article 14 repeats an ideal proposed over a century ago that "all the faithful should be led to that full, conscious and active participation in liturgical celebrations... (such participation) is the primary and indispensable source from which the faithful are to derive the true Christian spirit."[3]

These three truths officially proclaimed by the Church — the necessity of faith, the presence of the Risen Christ, and informed active participation by the faithful — spawned from the 1960's onward enormous activities in every parish throughout the United States and, for that matter, around the world.

Those efforts produced great blessings, but, as we will see, created some burdens as well.

Blessings

Pastoral leaders, reflecting upon the Council's teaching came to these practical conclusions: the sacramental rituals are

---

[3] *Vatican Council II: The Conciliar and Post Conciliar Documents*, Austin Flannery, O.P., General Editor (Northport, NY: Costello Publishing Company, 1981 Edition). *Constitution on the Sacred Liturgy*, Articles 59, 7, 14.

not mere magical moments, but must be acts of faith; participants need to be informed, understanding clearly what is happening during the sacred rites; parish leaders should facilitate the active involvement of everyone present for the liturgical celebration.

To achieve those goals, parishes began to develop and insist upon participation in *preparation programs* for the various sacraments.

> ➤ Parents seeking baptism of an infant are expected to be present for a session, sometimes several sessions, of education and inspiration. Most often a lay person, a couple, or a team of laity conduct this formation event.
> ➤ Recognizing that parents are the first and best teachers of the faith, many churches have fashioned programs preparing young children for First Penance and First Eucharist in which the father and mother are the primary instructors.
> ➤ Parishes, following diocesan guidelines, frequently shifted the age of Confirmation from elementary to high school levels. In such programs candidates for that sacrament generally follow a two-year process. During those 24 months they seek to prepare their heads (catechetical opportunities), their hearts (prayer and retreat experiences) and their hands (projects of service to the community and especially those in need).
> ➤ Couples approaching a church for the sacrament of matrimony are often afforded several preparatory options: weekend Engaged Encounters, diocesan Pre-Cana events or parish based marriage preparation experiences.
> ➤ Bereavement committees call upon grieving families to assist them in planning the funeral liturgies and even providing a luncheon for them at the parish center following the service.

These preparation programs, together with a host of other parish activities, generated an incredible explosion in the number of lay people actively serving as full or part-time, paid, or more often, volunteer church workers.

Those experiences brought enormous blessings to the teachers as well as the taught, to the servants and the served alike.

Concurrent with the rapid introduction and growth of these preparation programs was the remarkable popularity and impact of several *conversion experiences*. Some were already in existence; others emerged during those post-Vatican II days.

The Catholic Charismatic Renewal, Christ Renews the Parish, Cursillo, Marriage Encounter and Renew were a few of the major experiences; but there were others.

Even though they possessed different goals and followed distinct processes, there generally was a common result: participants experienced something of a spiritual conversion or radical change of heart. Those away from church for a long time came back to God and to Mass; those lukewarm, hit or miss Sunday Catholics became regular weekly Mass goers; those already faithful to worship, but not very active, became more so; the intensity of interest in prayer, religion and church rose significantly.

Both these preparation programs and conversion experiences were great blessings. But they produced some pastoral burdens as well.

Burdens

The conversion experiences made for a sudden and sizeable influx of committed persons into the parish. They were dedicated to the Lord, to the Church, and to their particular cause. These "graduates" became active members of the parish and many quite naturally assumed leadership roles in their faith committees.

That obviously was a tremendous benefit and blessing. But there was a downside to the phenomenon.

Persons who have undergone conversion experiences and are deeply committed, sometimes, in their enthusiasm, insist that everyone else be equally committed and even pressure them in that direction.

"Have you been saved?" "Do you have a personal relationship with Jesus?" "Were you baptized in the Spirit?" "Don't you speak in tongues?" "You must make a Marriage Encounter (or Cursillo or whatever)."

This insistence that everyone be equally committed, obviously a noble ideal, can clash with the Church's more flexible and gentle approach, as we will see in a moment.

The preparation programs likewise developed some negative side effects.

Every human policy or process, however beneficial and even necessary in the beginning, tends eventually to become somewhat rigid and unbending, often failing to change with shifting circumstances or even resisting exceptions in individual conflicts. That has become the case in some parish situations.

Moreover, a subtle and unhealthy theological attitude arose over the years. The sacraments seemingly became a reward for completing the necessary program, rather than a gratuitous gift from God. The requirements were now an obstacle to sacramental encounters rather than a process enriching these events. As a veteran pastor once remarked: "The sacraments are meant to help us be better, not a reward for being good."

The demand that everyone possess an intense level of commitment and the reluctance to adjust in certain complex circumstances led in some locales to general rules of this type: Regular Sunday Mass attendance and actual registration in the parish are requirements for baptism or marriage.

Such demands were perceived as rigidity and sometimes

hurt or angered petitioners, but also ran contrary to the Church's directives in these matters.

The late biblical scholar Father Raymond Brown once remarked: "The number of people who have turned away from the Church because they found it too forgiving is infinitesimal; the members who have turned away because they found it unforgiving are legion."

In the same vein, Avery Cardinal Dulles observed: "To large numbers of young people, and to others not so young, the laws and dogmas of the Church seem designed to control and crush rather than to nourish and satisfy the needs of the spirit."

Faithful and Firm, Flexible, Kind and Gentle

How do we compare requirements of regular Mass attendance and specific parish regulations for baptism and marriage to the Church's official approach?

It is *faithful and firm*.

The Church obviously stresses the supreme dignity of the Eucharist, the serious responsibility to attend Mass each week and the importance of good example on the part of parents.

Moreover, it encourages Catholics to become enrolled and active members of their parish.

The Church, in summary, seeks to teach what Christ taught, to proclaim the ideal and to challenge its members to strive for holiness through frequent participation in Mass and active involvement in parish life.

It is, at the same time, *flexible, kind and gentle*.

The Church also recognizes the frailty of its members, the weakness of human nature, and the complexities of daily life. Its rules uphold a lofty goal, but are, perhaps surprisingly to some, extremely flexible.

In chapters 6-8 on the sacraments of life and love, we will discuss in detail how regular Mass attendance, while desirable, is not a requirement for parents who seek to have their child baptized or for couples contemplating marriage. For baptism the Church requires only an assurance that the child will be raised Catholic; the couple anticipating marriage should intend to "commit their whole lives in unbreakable love and unconditional faithfulness by an irrevocable nuptial covenant."

The *Code of Canon Law* specifically reflects that same flexibility in some of its legislation. For example, it indicates that the pastor as shepherd has a responsibility to exercise pastoral care in the community entrusted to him. As a general rule, parish boundaries are territorial. Thus, those living within its limits have the right and responsibility to receive their sacraments, including baptism and marriage, in that church. Actual parish registration, while desirable, is not an indispensable requirement (Canons 518-519).

An Inclusive Church

The questions posed at the beginning of this chapter were almost rhetorical. It should be almost obvious that the Catholic Church, from top to bottom, is an inclusive Church. All of its members share an ambivalence which, as we have already noted, Jesus described in Gethsemane: "The spirit is willing, but the flesh is weak" (Matthew 26:41).

The late Monsignor Philip Murnion, visionary director of the Parish Project sponsored by the National Conference of Catholic Bishops and founder of the National Pastoral Life Center in New York City, summarized the inclusive nature of the Church in this way: "There are halfhearted and wholehearted members;

there are sinners and other trying to be holy; there are lukewarm Catholics and hot Catholics."[4]

The Church has always been able to embrace these disparate elements and yet, at the same time, within that inclusiveness, to keep posing the ideal and offering examples or models of virtue that all its members should strive to imitate in their lives. In a word, it is flexible, kind and gentle, but faithful and firm as well.

---

[4] Joseph M. Champlin, *The Marginal Catholic, op. cit.*, Chapter 4, pp. 47-64. The earlier quotes from Father Raymond Brown and Avery Cardinal Dulles are taken from p. 62 of that book.

CHAPTER THREE

LIFE AND LAWS

Imagine that you are the principal of a large elementary public school. At the middle of a near-zero winter day, the fire alarm sounds. Administrators, faculty and students bundle up and march outdoors.

In the meantime, the custodians locate the problem — no fire, but a fault in the alarm system.

School rules require that the students remain outside until the local volunteer fire department arrives, checks the building and approves re-entry.

There is a ten minute wait for the vehicles and fire fighters.

As the principal, would you keep the shivering students out in the cold, as the regulations dictate, or, in view of the harsh weather and the custodian's assurance that the building is safe with no fire, order their immediate return at least into the corridors of the school?

This case study or challenging situation illustrates a certain tension between laws and life.

We might detail that tension or conflict with the following, somewhat sobering truths:

First, civil laws are the products of limited and flawed human minds. Consequently, no legal decree is perfect.

Second, laws tend to lag behind life; legislation cannot keep pace with society's ceaseless behavioral shifts or people's constantly changing customs.

Third, laws are never able to adequately cover every individual case or circumstance.

The school regulations cited above would seem to fall under the first and third truths.

Civil Legal Systems

Two contemporary legal systems with which we are familiar — the European, Roman or civil law and the Anglo-American, English or common law — seek to deal with those sobering truths.

Both share the view that a system of laws accepted, understood and obeyed by members of a particular society or community is good, and more, is necessary for society's survival. They protect the rights of individuals; they enable citizens or members to live in peace and harmony; they promote the common good and the goals which that society, community or organization seeks to obtain.

Each system, however, while trying to achieve the purposes of good laws, attempts simultaneously to make provisions for the limitations of every legislative enactment, but in quite different ways.

The *European, Roman or civil law* system is based on the legal traditions, concepts and vocabularies of ancient Rome. At one time, mainly for commercial reasons, there was a search to discover some arrangement of rules applicable to all the persons of diverse origins living in the Roman Empire. Leaders sought to determine what principles might be common to every legal system. If these could be established, then, in their view, a perfect, universal set of laws would be possible.

This led to an approach which drafted legislation and built up a comprehensive system of laws that centered around major principles rather than detailed rules.

It enshrined generic values instead of proposing specific regulations.

In the European or Roman judicial approach, the judge studies the sweeping, universal and timeless law, then applies, adapts and interprets it to particular circumstances.

The *English, Anglo-American or common law* system began in England. The common law in England was the judge-made law which developed in the central or royal courts and was common to all of England. Characteristically, English and American law is made by judges deciding disputes on a case-by-case basis. The decision in a previous case becomes precedent or authority which judges normally follow in subsequent cases. While judges in European civil law courts sometimes arrive at unique solutions to the disputes before them, their decisions do not create new law. Rather, they purport to be interpreting and applying the general principles and rules of the civil code. Common law judges, in contrast, often make decisions which themselves establish principles and rules to be applied in future cases.

Flexibility, as well as consistency, is important in any legal system. The Anglo-American, common law systems achieve flexibility by giving judges the power to develop new rules or precedents as new and different problems are presented in the courts. The judges also have the power to abandon old precedents or rules established in earlier cases. Consistency is achieved in the common law systems because judges normally follow precedent, that is, the rules established in their own previous decisions, but they also have the power to change these rules when they do not fit the situation presented in court.

European law achieves continuity and flexibility in a different way. The written law sets forth principles and rules designed to cover all situations that come before the courts. The judges do not have the power to change these principles and rules, but they are expected to be flexible in interpreting and applying them. In that fashion, the written law can be adapted to the human needs in the unique situations before the courts. The judges are expected to respect the spirit, rather than the letter of the law.

The Anglo-American or common law system prevails in countries among the western nations where English is the dominant language. That, of course, includes the United States and Canada. The state of Louisiana, however, is an exception, following the European or civil law. The European or civil law system prevails where the dominant language is one of the derivatives of Latin, but it also exists in other countries such as Germany, Russia, Holland, Austria and Japan.[1]

The Church's Legal System

The Catholic Church is a community, a group of people who are believers. Like any community it requires some system of laws and regulations for the good of all.

That system naturally seeks as its fundamental basis the Hebrew Scriptures or Old Testament and the Christian Scriptures or New Testament.

In Judaism, law was a central factor, binding members to members and members to God.

In Christianity, Jesus fulfills the Old Testament law and

---

[1] For a more detailed discussion of this entire topic cf. Joseph Champlin, *The Marginal Catholic, op. cit.*, Chapter 5, "Laws and Life."

prophets while the Gospels, especially Matthew, presents the law or commandments of Christ as a significant element of the Good News.

In the Acts of the Apostles and the letters to Christian communities we read of discussions, debates and decisions about various religious matters.

For the first six Christian centuries there were many and varied laws or decrees covering a whole host of situations. Pope Gelasius summoned Dionysius, a monk from southwestern Russia, to Rome assigning him the task of collecting and systematizing all these legal texts into an organized body. These collections of "canons" (coming from the Greek for "rule") included norms for every facet of the Church's life.

In the twelfth century, Gratian, a professor at the University of Bologna, assembled all those existing canons into an orderly system of jurisprudence. That text, called the *Decretum*, became the resource for all persons involved in canon law.

There were continued developments in the Church's legal system over the next eight centuries, which reached a culmination in the early 1900's when Pope Pius X appointed Cardinal Pietro Gasparri to undertake the arduous task of assembling a code of law resembling the Napoleonic codes quite common in Europe. The result was the *Code of Canon Law*, published in 1917, arranging 2414 canons in a single book divided into five sections.

Recognizing the constant changes in society and the Church, Pope John XXIII called for a revision of the 1917 code. Pope Paul VI carried on the work which was completed in 1983 when Pope John Paul II issued the new *Code of Canon Law*. Moreover, Pope John Paul II, in 1990, promulgated the *Code of Canons of the Eastern Churches*.

It should be noted that Pope John Paul II, during this process of revision, frequently called for a new perspective or new approach to law which "would make law a more vibrant and pastoral tool in the Church."[2]

Comparing Civil and Church Law

The legal system in the United States, except in Louisiana, is based on the English, Anglo-American, common law approach.

It tends to be extremely complicated, even confusing and yet quite versatile. It is fluid, constantly shifting, efficient and flexible. General principles are revered, but limited in number. Statutes abound and are amended frequently. Legislation is often detailed, anticipating as many contingencies as possible. The result is an extremely active legal system, consisting of a complex, though manageable succession of laws and jurisprudence.

The Church law system, on the other hand, is based upon the European, Roman, civil law concept.

It tends to be clear and simple. It emphasizes written principles which are less complex, but not as flexible as civil laws. They are not easily or often changed. Instead, they need interpretation and application to achieve their purposes.

We can see these fundamental differences reflected in the published volumes of existing laws within both systems and illustrated by the quantity of books in the office of a judge or on the shelves of a bishop.

The number of tomes containing current civil laws, cases and interpretations in the office of a lawyer, judge or professor will overwhelm an uninitiated visitor.

---

[2]   Kevin E. McKenna, *The Ministry of Law in the Church Today* (Notre Dame, IN: University of Notre Dame Press, 1998), Chapter One, pp. 9-14. I have relied heavily upon Father McKenna's text for this summary of "The Church's Legal System."

On the contrary, the office of a priest or bishop would customarily contain as a legal reference only the Church's basic body of legislation, the 1917 and now the 1983 *Code of Canon Law* plus perhaps a sizeable commentary. Both codes are published in relatively small bound books. The 1983 edition, for example, contains less than 2,000 canons which touch nearly every structure of the Roman Catholic Church. Moreover, many of these are not statutes or laws strictly speaking, but more exhortative or theological statements.

All of this has practical ramifications for us as Catholics living in America. We inherit and imbibe the Anglo-American system of law. That means we are inclined to manifest great and sometimes an almost exaggerated respect for the law. Moreover, we also disdain those who seek exceptions or exemptions. We expect legislation to cover every aspect of life and normally do not violate even lesser civil legislations without inner anxiety.

Laws, therefore, are sacred for us. We do not lightly disobey or disregard them.

Nevertheless, canon law has been constructed according to the European or Roman, not the English or Anglo-American legal system. Interpreting Church law from the English or Anglo-American viewpoint tends to surround Church regulations with an inappropriate rigidity. Furthermore, only with reluctance do we accept exceptions or applications which are an essential part of all European or Roman law.

Church Law Flexibility

We have already seen in this book a few examples of flexibility in official Church laws and regulations. There will be many more illustrations in the chapters to follow.

In addition, however, under both the 1917 *Code of Canon*

Law and the modernized 1983 version the Church has always offered *legal exceptions, adaptations or exemptions* to existing norms.
While upholding the law, thus maintaining the principle of consistency and truth, the Church still recognizes the uniqueness of
each human situation and legalizes various ways of relief from
the law in those circumstances, thus manifesting the principle of
compassion and mercy. These ways of relief include:

- *Matters of minimal significance.* There is a Latin canonical
  axiom which traces its origin back to Roman law: *De mi-
  nimis non curat praetor.* Laws or norms as well as judges or
  officials should not be concerned about negligible matters
  or issues of minimal significance. That might be translated
  into the earthy adage: "Don't sweat the small stuff."
- *Nature of the document and directives.* Current Church liturgical law appears in many forms, some binding, some not.
  Moreover, such norms originate from sources of varying
  importance. A regulation in the ritual book, to illustrate,
  carries more weight than a private response from a Vatican
  office to a local bishop on a specific matter.
- *Custom and usage.* Both the 1917 and the 1983 *Code of
  Canon Law* state that local custom or usage is the best in-
  terpreter of laws. While the canons limit the development
  of legal customs, factual custom — the actual practice of
  the Spirit-guided community — helps underscore the fact
  that such a way of acting can be the clearest sign of what
  may be needed for Church order and discipline.
- *Cessation of law.* While a law may lose its binding force
  through contrary legal customs or by the introduction of
  new law, canonists agree also that when a Church law, canon
  or decree has become obsolete or useless, it is no longer a law.
  Although arbitrarily invoking this principle can be perilous
  for order in the Church, its existence does underscore the

need for community acceptance of Church law.

- *Dispensation from the law.* The Second Vatican Council introduced a movement toward subsidiarity or decentralization in the Church. A practical effect of this was to expand the power of the local bishop to dispense from the general law of the Church in particular cases which would benefit the spiritual good of the faithful.

  This relaxation of a merely ecclesiastical law in a particular case, done for the spiritual good of the faithful, extends to all disciplinary laws except a few which are reserved to the Apostolic See. For validity the dispensation requires a just and reasonable cause.

- *Epieikeia.* This hard to translate Greek word appears in Paul's Letter to the Philippians. He says to them, "Your kindness should be known to all" (Philippians 4:5). Instead of kindness, other translations read considerateness, forbearance, fairness, gracious gentleness or softness.

  The Greeks said that *epieikeia* should enter when strict justice becomes unjust because of its generality. "There may be individual instances when a perfectly just law becomes unjust or where justice is not the same thing as equity." A person who has the quality of *epieikeia* knows when not to apply the strict letter of the law, when to relax and introduce mercy.

  Aristotle introduced this idea in the context of his reflections on justice in the *Nicomachean Ethics*. By its very nature any law may in some cases produce imperfect justice or no justice at all. All law is universal; but about some things it is not possible to make a universal statement which shall always be correct. The scope of *epieikeia* "is to bring a corrective into the application of law whenever it is so warranted."

  In the Church, *epieikeia* is not invoked by Church

authority, but by those who are trying to observe the prescriptions of Church discipline. It has been defined as a "correction or emendation of a law which in its expression is deficient by reason of its universality, a correction made by a subject who deviates from the clear words of the law." To make such judgments and act upon them may be an act of virtue, discerning the deeper purpose of Church discipline.

Epieikeia is not only a hard word to translate, but a difficult notion to grasp. Furthermore, it also involves seeking to understand the mind or interest of the legislator.

A practical example may illustrate this point. A red light at 3:00 a.m. orders me to stop. However, there are absolutely no other vehicles within miles. *Epieikeia* tells me to run the red light, understanding that the legislator would never have intended for me to wait for 90 seconds until the green light appears.

- *Excusing cause.* Long before the Second Vatican Council, canon lawyers and moral theologians recognized and taught how one might be "excused" from observance of Church law. Serious inconvenience or disproportionate damage could make it morally impossible to keep a specific law and, thus, the person would be excused from it.

Moreover, several *long-standing Church axioms* offer additional reasons why and how parish clergy and pastoral leaders may and should be kind and gentle in their response to people's requests.

- "The salvation of souls… must always be the supreme law" (Canon 1752).
- If in doubt, judge in favor of the person.
- The sacraments are for the good of the people. *Sacramenta sunt proper homines.*

- In Church laws, "favors are to be multiplied; burdens are to be restricted."
- The sacraments not only presuppose, but also strengthen and deepen faith.

Interpretation and Adaptation

Since Church or canon law more closely resembles European civil law, Church officials like bishops or pastors ought not apply it in the way our American culture and tradition deals with written or statutory law, that is, by looking to the letter, rather than the spirit. Instead, they need to recognize that all law requires flexibility, as well as consistency. European and Church law achieve the flexibility necessary to adapt law to human needs and circumstances by entrusting that task to the one applying the law — the bishop or pastor in the case of Church law — who is expected to look to the spirit rather than the letter.

The Church's legal system, therefore, offers many opportunities to demonstrate gentleness and kindness — through its wide variety of laws, through its different exceptions or exemptions and through its interpretation or application of existing legislation to particular cases. At the same time, it insists that these exceptions to the law not be done lightly or without proportionate reason. Church laws preserve the principle of consistency and truth, protect Church unity and concord, and promote a desired spiritual communion among Catholics throughout the world. Too easy departure from the law undercuts all of those good effects.

Pastoral leaders, especially the clergy, thus must serve, in a sense, as informed and benign judges within the Church's legal system. Following the example of judges in the European tradition of law, they must be aware of the law and its importance, but remain equally conscious of the law's limitations and the need for a wise, gentle application to individual cases. Furthermore, following that same parallel, they should remember that "the letter brings death, but the Spirit gives life" (2 Corinthians 3:6).

A correct understanding of the clergy's role as judges who benignly interpret and apply Church regulations according to the European or Roman legal system should help us accept diversity of pastoral interpretations and applications. Instead of expecting that all will decide cases in the same fashion, we must anticipate different judgments in different circumstances.

Sometimes one hears complaints about such differences in judgment, with the expressed desire for more uniformity. From all we have noted in this chapter, is it not clear that such an unbending, rigid and frozen approach is at odds with the European, Roman model of law? Some clergy in their judicial role will stress the value or virtue of fidelity, consistency and truth; others will apply the balm of flexibility, compassion and mercy. Both approaches have legal foundations. We need to develop a more tolerant attitude to the fact of divergent judgments.

Conclusion

The practical application of this discussion about life and law should be clear from these three actual experiences:

➤ Parents, for unknown but obviously important reasons, asked a priest or pastoral minister if two persons or godparents were needed for baptism. They were immediately informed that two were required.

The abrupt and inaccurate reply stunned and hurt the well-meaning and anxious parents. It dramatized Cardinal Egan's comments about wounded people saying, "They were unkind to us."

Concerned grandparents of this child later consulted their own pastor who gave them the correct information: only one person is required, although there may be two; one must be Catholic.

The swift and uninformed response about Church laws caused unnecessary pain.

➤ Some would argue that the principal in the situation at this chapter's beginning has the responsibility not only to keep the law, but also to make judgments adjusting the rules in special circumstances, to observe the spirit of the law (the welfare of the children), not simply the letter of the law (keeping the children outside in the cold). Once assured that there was no danger inside, the principal could have readmitted the youngsters to the more comfortable heated corridors, responding with explanatory justification later to the perhaps irritated fire chief and to the school administration questioning his decision and action.

➤ Pastor A judged that the couple seeking their child's baptism did not manifest sufficient assurances about the future Catholic upbringing of the infant, and declined to baptize at that time, sending them away.

The disturbed parents then sought out Pastor B who, while recognizing the weak religious practice of the parents, saw enough faith and good will to prompt a well-founded hope that the child would be raised Catholic. He baptized the infant.

Pastor A, hearing of this development and amazed by it, called the bishop.

The bishop, a wise official with years of experience, listened to the complaint and then asked Pastor A:

"Would you consider yourself a conscientious and informed pastor?"

"Well, yes, bishop."

"Would you consider Pastor B a conscientious and informed pastor?"

Surprised, Pastor A somewhat reluctantly admitted,
"Well, yes, bishop."

The bishop simply responded: "Thanks for calling!"

I have over the past two decades told that true story at
countless clergy gatherings, always receiving a loud laughter from
the group at the bishop's astute answer. The bishop saw both
men as good priests, one stressing fidelity and firmness, the other
reflecting flexibility and gentleness.

At a recent clerical session, however, the group responded
with dead silence to the story. That atypical response shocked
and puzzled me.

A few minutes later a younger participant explained: "It
wasn't funny. We have to insist that they live up to their duties
as Catholic parents. We should correct the lackadaisical attitudes
that have crept into the lives of Catholics. They need to get on
the train or get off the track. Better to have a smaller-but-purer
Church. We must speak with a clear and true voice of faith."[3]

It is that rather severe approach, quite contrary to what I
would judge Pope Benedict's firm, but kind and gentle attitude,
and, quite at odds with the Church's flexibility toward legislation,
which prompted me to write this book.

---

[3] David Gibson, *The Rule of Benedict* (San Francisco: Harper Collins, 2006), pp. 11-16. The
   younger priest's explanation echoed sentiments of some who commented with enthusiastic
   praise on the election of Pope Benedict XVI.

CHAPTER FOUR

GUIDANCE FROM THE BIBLE

In the recent past the letters WWJD became popular through-out the United States. They appeared on bracelets and bumper-stickers; they surfaced frequently in published articles and in people's conversations. The letters stand for "What Would Jesus Do?" or, in retrospect, what would he have done in certain situations.

That is a good question. After all, the Gospels tell us that Jesus is the way, the truth and the life. "No one comes to the Father except through me" (John 14:6). Moreover, a contemporary Catholic community of believers, building upon Christ's words, study a basic text entitled "The Way" written by their founder.

For example, how would Jesus respond to a couple who seldom attend Mass, have little or no connection with the parish, and seem quite immature who now seek to marry in the Church? Or how would he respond to parents who seldom participate and seem to possess only minimal understanding of the responsibilities which arise from the sacrament of baptism which they seek for their children?

An examination of both Old and New Testament texts will give us some insights into what Jesus would do when facing such challenges.[1]

---

[1] Joseph Champlin, *The Marginal Catholic, op. cit.*, Chapter 3, pp. 35-46, which offers a more detailed treatment of the biblical background on this topic.

Old Testament

- *A Jealous God.* The first testament, the Hebrew Scriptures, portray a God who seemingly does not tolerate marginal followers or lukewarm believers. Yahweh is "a jealous God" who demands the exclusive kind of allegiance which a spouse must have for a spouse. The Jewish insistence on strict loyalty to the one God grew out of a desire to distinguish Israel from her Near Eastern neighbors, all of whom worshiped a host of heavenly deities.

"You shall not worship any other god, for the Lord is the Jealous One; a Jealous God is he" (Exodus 34:14). So great was the danger of the chosen people being corrupted, absorbed or compromised by surrounding inhabitants that they were to make no agreements with them, destroy signs of their false worship and never intermarry.

Yahweh alone is God, a God who is one and holy; Israel must realize that it can serve no other.

Yahweh is the master of nature and history, a holy, living God, the one who gives rain and the increase in the world around us. This personal, jealous God is more than a force of nature to be appeased by magical rites (see also Deuteronomy 4:25, 6:15).

- *Slow to anger, rich in kindness.* That jealous God, however, while never allowing marginal loyalty, still always welcomes home those who sincerely repent of their infidelity. "The Lord, the Lord, a merciful and gracious God, slow to anger and rich in kindness and fidelity" (Exodus 34:7).
- *Gentle, patient servant.* There are four songs of the Suffering Servant or "Servant-of-the-Lord" oracles in the book of Isaiah (42:1-41; 49:1-7; 50:4-11; 52:13-53:12). These sections portray the ideal Servant of God whose consecration

to the divine will — even in the midst of immense sufferings — takes away the sins of many. Various interpretations have been offered as to the identification of this Servant. But according to New Testament and Christian tradition, these prophecies are seen as fulfilled, at least most perfectly and completely, in Jesus Christ.

In the first Song of the Suffering Servant, quoted below, we observe this ideal leader, the "chosen one," working to bring about a community of justice or holiness and doing so, among other ways, through prophetic teachings. Nevertheless, he accomplished that mission "modestly and quietly, not whipping people into conformity but transforming them interiorly."

> Here is my servant whom I uphold,
> my chosen one with whom I am pleased
> Upon whom I have put my spirit;
> he shall bring forth justice to the nations.
> Not crying out, not shouting,
> not making his voice heard in the street.
> A bruised reed he shall not break,
> and a smouldering wick he shall not quench,
> Until he establishes justice on the earth;
> the coastlands will wait for his teachings.
>
> (Isaiah 42:1-4)

- *The potter and clay.* The image of God as the potter and us as the clay occurs throughout scripture.

In the beginning, "the Lord God formed man out of the clay of the ground" (Genesis 2:7). After Jesus' coming, dying and rising, St. Paul mentions that the Savior's followers hold the glorious treasure of the Christian life "in earthen vessels, that the surpassing power may be of God and not from us" (2 Corinthians 4:7). In those contexts this image communicates the greatness of God and the fragileness of humans.

More to the point of our concerns, however, are the uses of the potter and the clay image in the prophets Isaiah and Jeremiah (cf. Isaiah 29:16; 45:9; 64:7; Jeremiah 18:1-10). The latter particularly employs that ancient image to demonstrate God's ability and desire to make or remold us as soon as we repent of our evil ways. Thus it indicates the importance of conversion, if we hope to receive God's blessing and graces. From contemporary experience we know that soft clay can be refashioned over and over again into something new, better and more beautiful; once hardened and baked, however, it becomes fixed. That parallel to the human heart should be obvious. Here is the passage from Jeremiah:

> This word came to Jeremiah from the Lord: Rise up, be off to the potter's house; there I will give you my message.
>
> I went down to the potter's house and there he was, working at the wheel. Whenever the object of clay which he was making turned out badly in his hand, he tried again, making of the clay another object of whatever sort he pleased.
>
> Then the word of the Lord came to me: Can I not do to you, house of Israel, as this potter has done? says the Lord.
>
> Indeed, like the clay in the hand of the potter, so are you in my hand, house of Israel. Sometimes I threaten to uproot and tear down and destroy a nation or a kingdom. But if that nation which I have threatened turns from its evil, I also repent of the evil which I threatened to do. Sometimes, again, I promise

to build up and plant a nation or kingdom.

But if that nation does what is evil in my eyes, refusing to obey my voice, I repent of the good with which I promise to bless it (Jeremiah 18:1-10).

We suggest, therefore, that while in the Old Testament there was no room for marginal believers, there were nevertheless frequent teachings about the possibility of repentance. God is even seen as eager to welcome back those who experienced a change of heart. Moreover, the Hebrew Scriptures point to the coming Messiah as one who will take a gentler, more modest and quiet approach to those who refuse or are reluctant to accept and follow his message.

New Testament

- *Servant of Yahweh.* At the baptism of Christ in Luke's account, a voice from heaven declared, "You are my beloved Son; with you I am well pleased."

Through this allusion to Isaiah 42:1, the evangelist is asserting that Jesus is the Servant of Yahweh, fulfilling the prophecies we cited in the previous section (Luke 3:21-22).

Later, when beginning his public ministry, Jesus entered the synagogue at Nazareth on the Sabbath day, "stood up to read and was handed a scroll of the prophet."

He unrolled the document and chose for his passage excerpts from Isaiah, chapter 61, starting with "The spirit of the Lord is upon me..." (Isaiah 58:6; 61:1-2). After finishing the proclamation, he sat down and said to all those in the synagogue, "Today this scripture passage is fulfilled in your hearing" (Luke 4:16-21). Jesus thus claims that he himself is the Servant of the

Lord, fulfilling all those prophecies and thereby inaugurating the messianic era. His mission, however, will be accomplished by pardon, healing and liberation.

- *The gentle, patient Savior.* In the 12th chapter of St. Matthew's Gospel, Jesus realized that the Pharisees were scheming to put him to death, and he thereupon withdrew from that place. He cured all who came for help, but warned his recipients not to make him known. The Gospel then goes on to state that "this was to fulfill the words spoken through Isaiah the prophet":

> Behold my servant whom I have chosen,
>   my beloved in whom I delight;
> I shall place my spirit upon him,
>   and he will proclaim justice to the Gentiles.
> He will not contend or cry out,
>   nor will anyone hear his voice in the streets.
> A bruised reed he will not break,
>   a smouldering wick he will not quench,
>   until he brings justice to victory.
> And in his name the gentiles will hope.
>   (Matthew 12:15-21)

Readers will recognize that quote from Isaiah 42:1-4 which we discussed under our treatment of the Old Testament. However, Matthew's citation does not correspond exactly to the Hebrew, the Septuagint or any one original version. It is the longest Old Testament excerpt in this Gospel and is used to suit the author's purpose. Matthew seeks here to emphasize the meekness of Jesus, the Servant of the Lord, and to foretell the extension of Christ's mission to the Gentiles.

The Savior will not contend or wrangle with people nor

speak with vengeful wrath or strident arguments.

He also will not cry out or cry aloud like a dog barks, or a drunk bawls or a discontented theater audience roars. Instead of quarrels and shouts, the Servant will be quiet, yet strong, who seeks to conquer by love, not by strife of words.

The Messiah will be gentle with the reed which is bruised and hardly able to stand erect; he will be equally patient with the weak wick whose light is but a flicker. The Christ seeks not to discourage, but to encourage, to heal the crushed reed and nourish it back to health, to nurse the faint flame until it becomes strong and bright.

- *The wheat and the weeds.* Only Matthew has this particular parable which Jesus taught:

> The kingdom of heaven may be likened to a man who sowed good seed in his field. While everyone was asleep his enemy came and sowed weeds all through the wheat, and then went off. When the crop grew and bore fruit, the weeds appeared as well. The slaves of the householder came to him and said, "Master, did you not sow good seed in your field? Where have the weeds come from?" He answered, "An enemy has done this." His slaves said to him, "Do you want us to go and pull them up?" He replied, "No, if you pull up the weeds you might uproot the wheat along with them. Let them grow together until harvest; then at harvest time I will say to the harvesters, 'First, collect the weeds and tie them in bundles for burning; but gather the wheat into my barn'" (Matthew 13:24-30).

The weeds sowed by the enemy would have been commonly understood by the people in Palestine at the time of Jesus. Sometimes translated in older versions as "cockle" or "tares," this weed called bearded darnel was a curse against which farmers in the Holy Land had to labor. In its early stages it so closely resembled wheat that it was impossible to distinguish one from the other. Moreover, as both darnel and wheat grew, their roots became intertwined to such a degree that they could not be separated without tearing up and ruining the good wheat.

As the harvest reached maturity, the darnel, called "bastard wheat" by the Jewish people because of its resemblance to wheat, changed to a slate-grey color. It then could be distinguished from the wheat. Moreover, the two needed to be separated because the darnel was slightly poisonous. It was known to cause dizziness and sickness and it produced a narcotic effect; even in small amounts, it had a bitter and unpleasant taste.

At the end, the darnel or weeds were usually separated out by hand, tied into bundles and burned for fuel.

Harvest is a common biblical metaphor for the time of God's judgment. The obvious meaning and commonly accepted interpretation of this parable, therefore, is that Christ was warning his disciples not to anticipate God's final judgment by a definitive exclusion of sinners from the kingdom.

- *Net full of fish.* Shortly after the story of the weeds among the wheat, Matthew offers this very similar parable:

  Again, the kingdom of heaven is like a net thrown into the sea, which collects fish of every kind. When it is full they haul it ashore and sit down to put what is good into buckets. What is bad they throw away. Thus it will be at the end of the age. The angels will go out and separate the wicked from the righteous and throw them into the fiery furnace, where there will be wailing and grinding of teeth (Matthew 13:47-50).

There were two main ways of fishing in Palestine — hand casting a net and dragging a net between two boats. In this parable the author envisions the latter approach, which would gather indiscriminately all kinds of fish. Some were clean and some unclean by Levitical standards. Moreover, the mix would be enormous, ranging from 24-153 types of fish in the Sea of Galilee alone.

The interpretation parallels that of the weeds and the wheat. The Church until the Second Coming, the end of the ages, or the Parousia will always include good, fully committed and bad, tenuously connected members. Judgment or separation of the two will come at the final moment, but this remains God's task. Until then, patience and preaching is called for.

- *Lost sheep, misplaced coin and prodigal son.* Luke's chapter 15 contains these three well-known parables of God's persistent search for the lost or strayed. It begins with the Pharisees and Scribes complaining for the third time in Luke that Jesus "welcomes sinners and eats with them" (Luke 15:1). They charged him with encouraging loose morals by associating too freely with those whose lives were not perfect. In their judgment, a believer's duty was to avoid anything or anyone who could soil his or her sanctity. Christ's response through these parables indicated that God's merciful love does not wait for the sinner's repentance, but actively seeks out her or his restoration.

Sheep tend to stay together, but in the mountainous regions of Palestine one of a flock could little by little nibble its way to an isolated, dangerous location of no return. It was the task of the good shepherd, who knew the sheep, to expend every effort at the end of the day to find and carry back the lost one to safety.

In the dark, windowless oriental houses a coin could be easily lost in the straw on the floor. A careful housewife would not rest until she found the missing item, even if it meant turning everything upside down.

Pastoral ministers who have struggled with marginal parents and children in religious education programs, including sacramental preparations for first Penance, Eucharist and Confirmation, will easily be able to identify with the arduous efforts of the conscientious shepherd and careful housewife. So, too, they should find inspiration in the patient, unconditional love of the forgiving father who welcomes back his lost son.

What would Jesus do or how would he respond to those people mentioned at the beginning of this chapter seeking baptism or marriage? Neither the Old nor New Testament provides a specific answer.

However, the biblical texts indicate that he would clearly teach the ideals of God's kingdom, urge then to stretch a bit, and explain the meaning of both sacraments with the responsibilities flowing from them. At the same time, Christ would practice patience with those who have failed to adhere perfectly to his teachings and be "rich in kindness" toward those who manifest a willingness to start over or change their lives.

Perhaps the best summary of what Jesus would do in such circumstances is that he would fulfill his role as Messiah, as the Suffering Servant predicted by Isaiah, not crying out, not shouting, in gentle fashion being very careful not to break the bruised reed or snuff out the smoldering wick.

CHAPTER FIVE

A JOURNEY OF FAITH

Charles de Foucauld was born in 1858 at Strasburg, France into an aristocratic family. His father and mother died when he was six, leaving him with a large fortune and a grandfather as his foster parent.

He lived and believed as a Catholic until his late teens and early twenties when he began to read the works of skeptical and unreligious writers. That led him into both agnosticism, doubting the existence of God, and a dissolute lifestyle.

"He spent money lavishly and wildly. He gambled, drank and ate without restraint. He entertained on a grand scale. He was overweight and overdressed. He entered into an alliance with a young woman named Mimi and tried to pass this mistress off as his spouse. He was, in short, an aimless and purposeless young man."

However, journeys to North Africa and the Holy Land exposed him to believing Muslim and Jewish people. Their faith practices touched Foucauld, prompting him on his return to France to make a confession and begin a life of serious prayer.

Nevertheless, he struggled mightily with faith and whispered over and over what he termed his strange prayer: "O God, if you exist, make your presence known to me."

Eventually, he returned to an isolated spot in the desert

of northern Africa for prayer, writing, and the service of three tribes in the area. In 1916 he was murdered by a hostile group of natives.

Years after Foucauld's death his writings and example have inspired countless people to walk in the footsteps of this holy man. He was beatified on November 13, 2005 in Rome and declared to be Blessed Charles de Foucauld.[1]

The faith with which Blessed Charles struggled naturally received the attention of the bishops at the Second Vatican Council. As we have already seen, they declared that the sacraments "not only presuppose faith, but by words and objects they also nourish, strengthen and express it. That is why they are called 'sacraments of Faith'."[2]

Truths of the Faith

Roman Catholics are expected to believe explicitly or implicitly all the truths of the faith. Articles of the Nicene Creed recited each Sunday express in explicit fashion the major truths, for example, the Trinity, Jesus Christ, and the Resurrection. It does not mention other significant truths, for example, the Eucharist and the sacraments. However, those are expressed in implicit fashion within the Creed as it states that we believe in the Holy Catholic Church, thus emphasizing all the truths the Church teaches.

---

[1]   Joseph M. Champlin, *What It Means To Be Catholic* (Cincinnati: St. Anthony Messenger Press, 1987) pp. 32-33; Kate White, "The Hidden Life of Charles de Foucauld," *National Catholic Reporter*, November 11, 2005, pp. 13-15; Robert Ellsberg, "Evangelism of Presence," *America*, November 14, 2005, pp. 10-12; Robert Ellsberg, *All Saints* (New York: Crossroad Publishing Company, 1998), pp. 524-525.

[2]   *Vatican Council II, op. cit., Constitution on the Sacred Liturgy*, Article 59.

During the Rite of Baptism we see illustrated that explicit and implicit belief in the truths of the faiths. The celebrant asks for a threefold profession of faith from the parents and god-parents. These "Do you believe in..." questions include God the Father, Jesus Christ the Son, and the Holy Spirit as well as the holy Catholic Church. After their "I do" to each inquiry, the celebrant and the entire congregation give their assent to those professions of faith.

> This is our Faith. This is the Faith of the Church. We are proud to profess it, in Christ Jesus Our Lord.[3]

The "I do" and the celebrant/congregation's assent to those truths represent an inner and individualized faith.

The *Catechism of the Catholic Church* defines that interior, personal *faith* as a "gift of God, a supernatural virtue infused by him."[4]

An Interior and Personal Faith

All ultimate realities of life like God, love and death defy definition. Faith is one of them. We can't define, but only describe them, merely dance around those realities a bit, and arrive at but a partial understanding of them.

However, our now deceased former Ordinary of the Syracuse diocese, Bishop Frank J. Harrison, once offered a most useful description of faith. Faith, he maintained, is that which enables us to look beyond and see something more.

---

[3] *Rite of Baptism for Children* (New York: Catholic Book Publishing Company, 1976), Articles 58-59.

[4] *Catechism of the Catholic Church, op. cit.*, Article 153.

Here are ways that the notion of faith as looking beyond, seeing more, has universal appeal and, in addition, includes other situations that would apply only to Roman Catholics.

Beauty: Looking beyond a beautiful sunset, fall foliage or a star-filled sky can lead us to the God of all creation.

Burdens: Looking beyond a cancer diagnosis, marital disruption or job termination may help us discover the God who is close to the broken hearted and near to those who are crushed in spirit.

Blessings: Looking beyond our prayerful petitions and healing touches for an ill person could bring us to experience the meaning of Jesus' words in Mark's Gospel that those who believe will "lay hands on the sick and they will recover" (Mark 16:17-18).

Coincidences: Looking beyond large and little positive coincidences (how a couple met and married, or how a seemingly chance encounter resolved a particular challenge) often enables us to discover the presence of an awesome, but a loving God in our midst.

Rainbows: Looking beyond rainbows (which only occur in connection with a storm and dark clouds) may prompt us to remember the promise to Noah that this heavenly bow in the clouds is a pledge of God's everlasting covenant, love and concern for us on earth (Genesis 9:1-17).

These five "look beyond" possibilities clearly enjoy universal appeal. But Roman Catholics, in addition to these five, can with faith look beyond other signs or symbols and discover the Risen Christ.

In Article 7 of the *Constitution on the Sacred Liturgy*, as we have also noted, the bishops taught that Christ is always present in his Church, especially in her liturgical celebrations.

Then in rather staccato fashion the document cites how the Risen Jesus is present in the Eucharist particularly, but in other sacraments as well, when the scriptures are proclaimed, and when the Church prays and sings.

It obviously requires an interior and individualized faith to look beyond these natural and supernatural realities to recognize God the Creator and the Risen Christ dwelling among us.

The Journey of Faith

The word "conversion" in the past has been used most often to describe a person's change from one religious tradition to another. We say that they converted to Catholicism or are converts to an evangelical church.

In current Roman Catholic practice, we generally avoid the terms "converts" or "conversion" in that regard. Instead we speak of catechumens (those who have never been baptized) or candidates (those who were baptized in another Christian tradition). They enroll in the Rite for the Christian Initiation of Adults and, usually at the Easter Vigil, are baptized and/or received into the Church as well as confirmed.

The term "conversion" is employed in a much wider context and includes various types of turning points in people's lives.

Conversions are not magic moments, but human processes. They may occur in an instant or over a long period. They normally are more complex and more involved than a simple event or a movement in time. They involve duration and continuity. Conversions involve not only a single event, or a number of isolated events, but a series of related events played out over a span of months or even years. They involve not only the events, but the people in the events, and all that they go through as they experience the events described. They involve time, change and growth.

Conversion can denote the turning from no religion to some

religion, from no belief to some belief, from a sinful, destructive way of life to a virtuous, constructive manner of living, from being an inactive Catholic to becoming an active one, from routinely carrying out one's religious duties to doing so with fire-fervor, from leading a good life to leading an even better one.

There are two key words in this conversion or turning experience as applied to sacramental encounters in general and baptism or marriage in particular: personal and process. Each conversion is, or at least should be, totally personal, unique, individual. Each case is different, every person follows a singular journey. Moreover, each conversion entails a process which takes time and travels an uneven, not always direct or ever-forward path.

These personal and process components of conversion require both respect and patience from those in pastoral ministry, who need to respect the Holy Spirit's gentle, often surprising and hidden movement within the hearts of people. In addition, there is a great need for patience, for understanding that journeys of faith move at their own frequently slow pace and usually cannot be hurried.

Some persons never move beyond the faith of a child or youngster; others grow gradually and arrive at a very mature faith level; still others practice faith, then let it lie dormant, and finally through various events leap forward to a new stage in their faith development.

Priest confessors, better perhaps than anyone else, can testify to this, particularly at special moments of reconciliation like Christmas or Easter. Penitents away for years from the Church, Mass and Communion, approach the sacraments. What brought them to this new awareness or fresh rediscovery of their faith? It may be the death of one they love, the approaching First Communion of a child, a major moral lapse which jolted their conscience, a bitter disappointment, or the boredom of mid-life.

For some, there is no such event or circumstance, but rather a gradual stirring of the heart. Those Spirit-given impulses frequently will bring the person back to Sunday Mass for several months, or even years, before taking that final step of confession or reconciliation.

The phases of believing and practicing one's beliefs thus often may alternate between moving ahead and slipping behind, between being apparently at one moment on fire with faith and at another time wearied or bored by the whole spiritual struggle. The challenge for pastoral leaders in the Church is to accept at whatever level of faith people are, and to give them reason to build and grow.

My own experiences and many conversations with clergy, both in the United States and in Canada, indicate that major conversions in terms of returning to full, active participation in the life of the Church *do not* come for most couples at their wedding or at the baptism of their first child (children). While those occasions, handled well pastorally, can keep alive their flickering faith and perhaps enkindle it a bit, the major turning point seems generally to occur when the initial youngster nears the age for First Communion. That not infrequently coincides with the parents' arrival at their late twenties and early thirties — statistically significant times for a return to earlier faith values and practices.

Becoming a Catholic Christian means embarking upon a journey of faith which is ongoing, lifelong, very personal, individualized, uneven, and often plagued with interruptions, detours and sometimes even disasters. And the journey is not over, until it is over.[5]

---

[5] Joseph Champlin, *The Marginal Catholic, op. cit.*, pp. 20-33.

Judging About Faith

Pastoral ministers face a daunting task. They have a responsibility to challenge those who are seeking the sacraments or liturgical services: Do they have at least the minimal faith required? Are they aware of both the sacrament's meaning and the responsibilities which go with it? Will they fulfill those duties?

At the same time ministers need to be kind, gentle and flexible, careful not to crush the well-meaning, even though sometimes careless or non-practicing Catholics who approach them.

I want to explore that "challenge, yet don't crush" tension.

First the "challenge." We have seen that the Church insists that the sacraments require, presuppose and demand faith. Moreover, Church teaching frequently stresses that the effectiveness of a liturgical rite requires the people's full, conscious, and active participation in it. In addition, if the Eucharist especially is at the center of Catholic spiritual life, everything should lead to and flow from the Mass. Finally, the liturgy is meant to be a communal or community celebration, not a private or individualized event; every liturgical service should involve the entire Church.

Of course, it is also presumed or at least hoped that the liturgical celebration will, as it were, work: the child will be in fact raised Catholic, the confirmed young people will continue their religious duties and service of others, and the married couples will remain faithful and fruitful.

During the preparation for these celebrations, pastoral ministers need to effectively communicate these ideas and describe these duties to those seeking the Church's sacraments. Thus they serve as teachers and motivators.

Now the "don't crush" dimension of such pastoral experiences. Faith, as we have seen, is a supernatural virtue, an interior, spiritual, personal quality. Can we really judge its presence or absence?

It is risky to make judgments about an individual's inner life. Only God can and may do that. "Stop judging, that you may not be judged" (Matthew 7:1). "Therefore you are without excuse, every one of you who passes judgment" (Romans 2:1). "The one who judges me is the Lord. Therefore, do not make judgment before the appointed time, until the Lord comes, for he will bring to light what is hidden in darkness and will manifest the motives of our hearts, and then everyone will receive praise from God" (1 Corinthians 4:4-5).

We believe the Church possesses a divine element not only because it enjoys Christ's presence and protection, but it also is concerned with people's relationship with God, with the spiritual or interior lives of human beings. Nevertheless, the Creator alone can penetrate the depths of every person.

> O Lord, you have probed me and you know me;
> you know when I sit and when I stand;
> you understand my thought from afar....
> Such knowledge is too wonderful for me;
> too lofty for me to attain.   (Psalm 139:1-2, 6)

Consequently, we should not, indeed, cannot, judge or measure the inner religious state of another individual.

But the Church as established by Christ also possesses a human element because it is made up of flesh and blood, spirit and body members. It forms a visible society or community with unique requirements for those who wish to enter, and especially given codes of conduct for those who belong.

However, those rules even though governing religious or spiritual activities, pertain essentially to a person's exterior life. While their observance ought to and normally does flow out of and reflect an individual's inner state, that connection is not automatic. It is a barometer of one's interior condition, but not necessarily an accurate and precise measure of the existence or degree of a person's faith.

Thus, we acknowledge the biblical injunction against judging and recognize our inability as human beings to evaluate the inner life of another person. Moreover, while understanding the need for certain regulations of behavior within the Church as indispensable for a visible society, we at the same time grasp the imperfect connection between those external actions and an individual's interior life.

During the preparation of *Faithful to Each Other Forever: A Catholic Handbook of Practical Help For Marriage Preparation*, the committee sent drafts to certain bishops for their input. One replied that Hispanics resent the idea of their faith being judged by attendance at Mass. Many in Latin America seldom had the opportunity of assisting at Mass regularly, much less every Sunday. Yet they believed, prayed and sought to live the Catholic faith.

We can ask then these questions:

What level of faith is needed for membership in the Church, for reception of a sacrament, for eternal salvation? What type of adherence to the Church's teachings is required to become a Catholic, to remain a Catholic, to be a faithful, good Catholic?

Guidance From Experienced Leaders

In resolving this complex and delicate "challenge/don't crush" tension, the following words from experienced pastoral leaders might prove helpful.

Pope John Paul II: Early in his pontificate, Pope John Paul II wrote of two principles or policies about these matters.

Consistency: which requires the Church and pastoral ministers always to speak the truth "whereby the Church does not agree to call good evil and evil good."

Compassion: through which the Church or a pastoral minister "ever seeks to offer, as far as possible, the path of return to God and of reconciliation... careful not to bend the bruised reed or to quench the dimly burning wick."[6]

Father Andrew Greeley, diocesan priest, sociologist and prolific author, urges pastoral ministers to "invite, charm and enchant the laity as they approach the sacraments instead of imposing rules and regulations, creating obstacles and demanding compliance."[7]

David Gibson, author, longtime employee of Vatican Radio, regular traveler with our late Holy Father, Pope John Paul II, observes "Life in the Christian community is always a tug-of-war between love and belief, between offering the limitless clemency of Christ and upholding the moral law that makes a community truly Christian. It is never easy; in fact, it is usually impossible. But that is the inherent tension of the Christian life, or any fully lived religious life. It is an ambiguity that the credible believer acknowledges in himself, and one that he allows for in others."[8]

Pope Benedict XVI: As we noted earlier, the Holy Father, celebrating his first anniversary as the Successor of Peter, expressed his desire to be a "firm, but gentle shepherd."

St. John Bosco, founder of the Salesians and dedicated to the young, wrote to his members with this advice for them as they worked with youth: "We must be firm, but kind, and be patient with them."[9]

---

[6] John Paul II, *Reconciliation and Penance*. Post Synodal Apostolic Exhortation, December 2, 1984 (Washington, DC: USCC Office of Publicity and Promotional Services, 1989), section 34.

[7] Andrew Greeley, *America*, November 20, 1999.

[8] David Gibson, *The Rule of Benedict, op. cit.*, p. 210.

Blessed Charles de Foucauld, after his conversion, led a holy life, but still struggled to believe. Clergy and pastoral ministers might offer both his personal journey and prayer for faith as encouragement to those experiencing similar challenges.

---

[9] *From a letter by Saint John Bosco, priest.* Taken from the "Office of Readings" on his feast, January 31, in *The Liturgy of the Hours* (New York: Catholic Book Publishing Corp., 1975), Volume III, pp. 1337-1339.

CHAPTER SIX

TEACHABLE AND TOUCHABLE MOMENTS

A journalist recently did a yearlong study of about a half-dozen well-known giant, full-service mega-churches throughout the United States.

Similar ingredients or phenomena greeted him at each of these massive communities: ample parking, clear signage, clean bathrooms, attractive landscaping, cordial greeters. A warm, but respectful and non-intrusive welcoming attitude. Singable music. Relatable sermons. Inclusive worship. Countless and diverse services responding to their members' needs.[1]

An engaged couple telephoned the bride's parish to set a date for their wedding. A receptionist reserved the day and time. Curiously, there was no subsequent and relatively immediate personal meeting with the prospective bride and groom.

Months later, with the reception details in place, the couple called the parish for some information. To their surprise and

---

[1] Judith Ann Kollar, *A User-Friendly Parish* (Mystic, CT, 1998), Foreword.

panic, they learned that not only had their reservation **not** been made in the wedding book, but another couple now had their date and time.

The parish people offered no help in trying to resolve this situation. The distressed couple was forced to check the yellow pages of the phone book for Catholic churches. They called 15 and received no positive responses or assistance of any kind.

Eventually, a priest did reply to their plight and later another one. Together they worked out a satisfactory solution for the beleaguered couple.[2]

The newly appointed rector of an East Coast cathedral, during his initial months, heard repeated complaints from local clergy about the music at diocesan functions celebrated in this cathedral church. In his first year as a rector, the priest made only minimal adjustments to the music program. He did, however, raise the maintenance budget and add a modest array of bushes and flowers around the front entrance. The cathedral looked more attractive on the outside and cleaner on the inside.

His clergy critics, curiously enough, now no longer complained about the music. Those basic user-friendly steps somehow dissolved their objections.

Lessons Learned

Lesson 1: A Catholic married couple, active parishioners, regular at Mass and extremely dedicated parents of several quite young children, experienced a very dark shadow in their lives.

---

[2] *Ibid.*

The crisis affected their relationship to God and they soon simply vanished from the parish's radar screen.

Two years later this couple surfaced as enthusiastic members of a mega-church in the area. All of those characteristics of a welcoming community mentioned above were present and seemed to meet their spiritual needs. They attended long services each week, sometimes even twice weekly, became involved members of the church and deeply immersed themselves with their children in the Bible.

Their religious journey from darkness and despair to light and love clearly contained many positive elements. They reunited with God in a personal way, are back at church for worship on a regular basis and sacred scripture has become a vital part of their lives.

But there are negative aspects from a Roman Catholic perspective. Why did they not find in the Catholic Church what was needed in their darkest hour? Will they miss Mary, the Mother of Jesus in their spiritual lives since that mega-church with all its warm and welcoming elements gives Our Lady at best minimal attention? How much will they realize that their new spiritual home has a much weaker Eucharistic belief and practice?

Lesson 2: The painful scenario for that engaged couple with the botched wedding reservation is a reminder about the riskiness of telephone responses to requests for major events such as baptisms, weddings, funerals or other church services.

While these may be routine matters for pastoral ministers, they are critical or crisis issues for the callers. This does not mean crisis in terms of a suicide or a 911 emergency message; it does signify, however, a crisis in that this request often contains beneath it a highly emotional content. The telephone call and the actual service sought are simply the point or the surface of the situation. Beneath that inquiry there will frequently be anxiety, doubts or nervousness as well as fears, questions or embarrassment.

Will they baptize our baby since we have seldom gone to Mass in the recent past? Will they refuse to marry us because we are living together now?

Our own life experiences have taught us how telephone exchanges can easily occasion misunderstandings. Moreover, we may say harsh things over the telephone which would be softened, clarified or avoided if we were communicating face to face.

Studies indicate that 55 percent of communication happens by visual means or by appearances. Folded arms, glances at one's watch convey one message; a broad smile and an erect, but relaxed posture convey something quite the opposite. The eyes, we have been told, are doorways to the soul.

Those same statistics indicate that 38 percent of communication occurs through the tone of one's voice. Identical words can convey very different meanings depending upon the way we speak them.

Only seven percent of communication depends on the actual content of the message.

The potential for misunderstanding and harm through a telephone exchange is so great and the possibility for good communication through a personal interview is so enormous that the latter is clearly the preference. In that situation we can see the others' faces, sense their feelings and catch the meaning behind the words spoken.

When Church personnel discuss baptism, marriage or similar matters in detail over the telephone with the interested parties, they tread a perilous path. The risks involved in such an approach are staggering. They would be well advised simply to listen carefully over the phone, exude loving warmth, offer no judgments or answers and request that, whatever the context, the callers come to the office where these always delicate matters can be discussed more fully and satisfactorily. The telephone exchange, then, merely identifies the issue, creates an initial positive atmosphere and arranges a future personal appointment.[3]

In addition to the frustration and pain those many fruitless telephone calls caused the couple, there are several additional lessons which we might take from that incident.

Mistakes like the neglected reservation will happen. In that particular circumstance, it is regrettable that the pastoral minister or parish clergy did not offer to help them find an alternative venue and suitable resolution. They would in that context admit the unintentional error and failure, but subsequently assist the traumatized individuals.

My experience with over 1,000 weddings in the past dozen years suggests that for a variety of very good reasons either the prospective bride or groom, usually the bride, should make the contact with the parish to arrange a wedding, rather than a parent.

A final point: the first personal interview with a couple is best done very soon after the initial phone call. Had this occurred with that unique, but unfortunate case, the tension, stress and pain the bride and groom experienced most likely would have been avoided.

Lesson 3: The pleasant and positive impact of new shrubbery on the outside and a cleaner church on the inside at that East Coast cathedral merely underscores the value of those various practices which the journalist found in all the mega-churches.

---

[3] Joseph M. Champlin, *The Marginal Catholic, op. cit.*, pp. 101-102.

The Miracle of Life and Baptism

A young New England priest frets about the baptism of children of parents who are marginal in the practice of the faith. "I worry about it day and night," he says, "and feel like calling the bishop or even the pope about this. Should I or should I not baptize this baby of parents who seldom are at Sunday Mass?"

His concern is noble and understandable, but, nevertheless, rather sad. Celebrating this miracle of new human life and new spiritual life, after all, should be a joyous event for all involved, including the priest or deacon who pours the holy waters. Moreover, regularly administering that sacrament of baptism ought to be a nourishing, not a worrisome experience for the clergy.

The testimonies of both physicians and parents confirm the miraculous nature of conception and birth as well as validating the teaching of the Church in this regard.

The bishops at the Second Vatican Council spoke of the marvelous link between a powerful God with a man and woman who together in this divine-human action create new life. Spouses cooperate, they taught, "with the love of the Creator and Savior, who through them will increase and enrich his family from day to day."[4]

The *Catechism of the Catholic Church* puts that truth in this way: "Human life is sacred because from its beginning it involves the creative action of God."[5]

A now deceased obstetrician who during his life delivered several thousand babies once commented, "Despite the many times I have done this, I never get over the miracle of it all."

A physician who has worked in emergency rooms for thirty

---

[4] *Vatican Council II, op. cit., Pastoral Constitution on the Church in the Modern World*, Article 50.
[5] *Catechism of the Catholic Church, op. cit.*, Article 2258.

years rarely delivers babies. However, in those few instances when he has, the doctor recalls, "I have never done so without tears."

During the baptismal homily, I ask the parents: "Do you remember what you felt when this baby came into the world?"

They reply with words or phrases like: "Joy, love, proud, happy, content, couldn't believe it, scared, a miracle, tired."

At the celebration of one baby who came into the world at 11 lbs. 6 ounces, the father said he felt extremely proud, but the mother simply commented that she felt *very* relieved.

For the parents this is what we might call a teachable and touchable moment. They are normally open to learning about the spiritual meaning of baptism. They also are eager to celebrate the joy of this new life. These parents sense, if only in an unconscious way, that they have cooperated with God in bringing marvelous new life into the world, a unique expression of their love for each other.

The Initial Contacts

- The first contact with a parish to arrange for baptism tends to be a routine matter for the church personnel, but, as we have seen, it is a crisis or critical event for the parent making the call.

Because of that importance and sensitivity, it would seem desirable to have the clergy or a well-trained pastoral minister respond to that contact rather than the parish receptionist who is too often busy with many concerns and phone calls of which this is but another. Under such pressure the possibility of a brusque reply or even communicating sometimes inaccurate information is real.

Connecting the petitioner immediately with the clergy or

designated pastoral minister is, of course, best. However, if that is not possible, the receptionist should simply inform individuals that a message about the baptism request will be left with the clergy or pastoral minister who will respond as soon as possible.

• The telephone return call could follow this pattern: "You called about baptism. Congratulations on the new baby, this miracle in your lives! How are you doing? And your spouse? Getting any sleep? We would be delighted to baptize the child. When can you, or your spouse or both of you come to the parish for ten minutes? We can then get the necessary information, set a time and date, as well as provide you with printed materials to help in the preparation for this celebration."

It is generally difficult for busy new parents and pastoral ministers to find one hour for an appointment. However, a 10-15 minute meeting is usually quite doable.

• For that subsequent short personal interview, a warm and cordial welcome clearly is critical. After preliminary greetings and personal admiration of the baby, the clergy or pastoral minister should find that questions like the following serve as great ice breakers and yet evoke significant replies. A Long Island priest with considerable Marriage Encounter experience developed them as a means of connecting this birth to their own marital relationship:

> How did you arrive at the baby's name?
> Has becoming parents affected your relationship as husband and wife?
> What are your hopes for this child?

Their response to the third question will usually focus on the natural or material level — e.g., education, career, marriage. The clergy or pastoral minister may then need to speak gently about the spiritual and religious upbringing of this baby.

- Completing a form with the necessary information — e.g., name, birth date, parents — will sometimes surface areas that need attention — e.g., marital status, godparents, and church attendance. The interviewer might make a mental note of those problematical circumstances, but postpone addressing them until after setting the date and presenting the materials.
- The printed items include Liguori's extremely attractive, informative and popular (over a million in print) *Your Baby's Baptism*, two copies of a form for sponsors, and a half dozen invitations.

A copy of "An Understanding and Agreement for A Sponsor or Godparent at Baptism or Confirmation" has been reprinted at the end of this book. It indicates the role, requirements and function of a sponsor or godparent with the Understanding and Agreement to be signed on the reverse side and a direction to return it one week beforehand. The requirements and function are taken from the *Code of Canon Law* and the *Rite of Infant Baptism*.

Using this document achieves two purposes: it informs the parents and through them the godparents of a sponsor's responsibilities; it also obviates the need of a recommendation letter from the sponsor's parish.

The invitations contain spaces to note the baby's name together with the date and time of baptism. Members of my parish team developed this invitation format for me thirty years ago and since then I have adapted and used it in two other churches, in-

cluding the Cathedral. Parents almost always react with pleasure
and surprise when I give them with explanation a half-dozen
copies and suggest that they duplicate extras if needed. A sample
likewise appears at the end of this book.

This process requires only 10-15 minutes, but it puts them
at ease, secures the information required and provides the parents
with useful materials.

With a pleasant and positive climate now established, the
clergy or pastoral minister then, if necessary, addresses those
delicate issues which may have surfaced at the start of the meeting.

Parish baptismal preparation programs, ideally with lay
leadership, build upon and complement this initial individualized meeting.

For over 15 years with more than 100 baptisms annually, I
have followed this process and found it pastorally very successful.
It eliminates the risks of an immediate telephone response. It creates a positive atmosphere when the clergy or pastoral minister
makes that initial contact. It resolves a practical challenge without imposing burdensome time demands upon all concerned. It
provides a setting in which the clergy or pastoral minister can
inform the parents (and indirectly godparents) of their spiritual
responsibilities. It establishes a suitable setting for the distribution
of materials that are well-received. In a remote fashion it prepares
for a more personal and active participation in the subsequent
celebration of the sacrament.

In a word, the process responds exceptionally well to this
critical, teachable, and touchable moment for parents seeking a
child's baptism.

The Wonder of Love and Matrimony

In clergy conferences during the past two decades I have regularly proposed this question to the participants: "How many of you would prefer to do ten funerals to one wedding?" Generally the vast majority immediately and somewhat emphatically raise their hands.

That response is understandable, but, as in the case of the New England priest mentioned earlier and his worries about baptism, it is also sad. Understandable, because in preparing for a funeral the deceased do not talk back and do not make insistent demands about the liturgy to be celebrated.

In the wedding experience, on the contrary, clergy and pastoral ministers must, among other challenges, deal with: cohabitating couples, religiously marginal brides and grooms, requests for bizarre music or major alterations in the nuptial liturgy itself and parents, particularly mothers, trying to dominate the event. In addition, at rehearsals they must cope with situations when the wedding party arrives late, or the couple has forgotten the license, or the participants simply are not cooperative with the clergy or pastoral ministers.

Nevertheless, that response of the clergy is sad because the bride and groom, regardless of all those possible negatives described above, have experienced the wonder of love. They have great dreams both about the nuptial ceremony and about their future as well.

It is also a teachable and touchable moment for the bride and groom. Simultaneously, it could be a satisfying and encouraging occasion for the clergy and pastoral ministers to witness a couple's unique love for each other and to share their excitement about the coming events.

We might in this context recall that Pope Benedict's inaugural encyclical was *Deus caritas est* or "God is love." After discussing at length *eros* or erotic love and *agape* or spiritual love, the Holy Father went on to examine "love of neighbor." He wrote: "I wish in my first Encyclical to speak of the love which God lavishes upon us and which we in turn must share with others."[6]

The First Connections

Everything we suggested about transferring the initial response to an inquiry about baptism to the clergy or delegated pastoral minister holds true, perhaps with even greater urgency, in the case of arranging the nuptial service. There are often so many potential and delicate circumstances involved that persons with experience, knowledge and skills — generally the clergy in these situations — are needed here.

Those individuals responding should communicate in a warm and welcoming manner, and then arrange for a personal meeting which will last for 1-2 hours to discuss details.

The mere reservation of a definite day and time for the formal meeting with the parish clergy will in almost all cases relieve the couple of the tension at this crisis moment. It means the process or journey to the altar has begun. They are now underway. The initial connection with the Church has been pleasant and positive.

We have thus quite easily created a climate or set an atmosphere for all the sessions which will occur in the months ahead.

In today's wedding liturgy, the presiding priest or deacon has a particularly important role to play. Since couples have the opportunity to select the readings, prayers and blessings they like

---

6   David Gibson, *The Rule of Benedict, op. cit.*, pp. 355-356.

as well as to incorporate certain creative elements of their own into the nuptial celebration, someone needs to blend together what might be disparate ingredients. The clergyman who will preside most easily fulfills that function. Because the bride and groom want their ceremony to move along smoothly and come off well, they recognize early on that the priest or deacon who will lead the liturgy is crucial for its success.

Moreover, first impressions are critical.

Linking those two items together — the significance of the presiding liturgist to the celebration's success and the power of initial impressions — prompts us to urge the priest or deacon who will preside at the liturgy to conduct the initial personal interview.

Other people will eventually become involved in the marital preparation process. Nevertheless, when the liturgical presider manages the initial interview well, he creates a close and respectful bond between himself and the couple which will prove highly beneficial later at the wedding rehearsal and nuptial service. They have come to know, like and trust him.

It is good for the priest or deacon involved in the initial encounter to recognize some obvious elements present which make this encounter such a critical occasion.

- *A major social event.* This is most likely the first time the couple have the dominant role in a major social event, the cost of which will range anywhere from $3,000-$50,000. The engaged pair of course, hope their total expenses will be closer to the former, rather than the latter figure. They want this major and uniquely significant experience to go well and are somewhat apprehensive about that.
- *Unfamiliarity.* For many and probably most couples, a personal interview with a member of the Catholic clergy will be a first ever experience, unexplored territory. Questions

like the following dominate their thinking: Where do we meet? What do we say? How do we dress? What will he say? Few people are totally comfortable with the unfamiliar. Probably the majority of persons, even those quite sophisticated, feel at least unsettled in these circumstances and some individuals may even be rather overwhelmed by the prospect.

- *Problematic circumstances.* When the couple brings with them any unusual problems, circumstances or requests, the level of anxiety normally rises. More common examples of these include: one or both have been previously married and divorced; they are already cohabitating; either or both have slipped from faithful church attendance; one is not Roman Catholic; the bride-to-be is pregnant; they wish something unique or special like being married in another location (e.g., in the bride's own Protestant church, or at a neutral site such as the local hotel because one spouse is Jewish) or having a clergy friend from outside witness the vows. In such situations they may nervously wonder beforehand: Will we be turned down because of the divorce(s)? Will he reprimand or reject us? Will my partner who is not Catholic like the priest or deacon? Will the pregnancy make a difference? Will he grant our requests and go along with our wishes?

- *Conscious or unconscious personal baggage.* With a 50% divorce rate, the high incidence of alcoholism and other addictions, an alarming incidence of domestic and sexual abuse, mental or emotional illnesses as well as other disturbing factors in today's society, many, perhaps most couples coming to arrange a marriage bring some conscious or unconscious baggage to the initial meeting.

- *Different expectations.* The clergy, familiar with the routine of arranging details of a marriage and perhaps struggling with the boredom of a task done so often, tend to be thinking about the couple's religious status, relationship with each other and attitude toward the sacrament of matrimony. The engaged pair, on the other hand, will be more concerned about the practical details of the wedding. Given today's difficulties with reserving a suitable place for the reception, their primary questions could be: Will we get the church for the date and time desired? After that, their preoccupation will usually center on externals such as: How do we contact the organist? Who will officiate? What are the costs? Where do we get the license? Must we attend classes? Is there a great deal of complicated paperwork? Until these concerns about pragmatic details of the wedding are answered and their attending anxiety relieved, the engaged pair will not hear much of what is said to them about relationships and religion.

- *The discomfort of a new relationship.* In addition to all the above factors, there remains the basic complexity of any three persons suddenly entering into any new relationship, in this case the couple with the priest or deacon. Sometimes the mix works immediately and well; at other times, the relationship is not so comfortable. There can be times when the chemistry among the three is instant and agreeable; at other times there may be personality clashes or temporary misunderstandings which leave all three uneasy. A certain discomfort is normal when strangers first meet, as they break through outer barriers, learn about one another and gradually develop a mutual trust which will sustain or even deepen the new relationship. Developing a cordial relationship in a relatively brief period of time takes energy, skill and willingness on the part of the priest or deacon. But even with the best of intentions, the clergy cannot expect that a warm, caring and close bond will emerge with every couple who seeks to marry in the Church. But at least efforts can be extended to be gracious with them and to provide the information or assistance they need. To recognize that even the most sophisticated couple will feel in all probability some discomfort at the initial meeting, could be the most essential step in establishing a cordial connection from the start.

Some Start-up Questions

As with parents seeking a baby's baptism, so, too, with an engaged couple requesting matrimony, some preliminary questions help put them at ease and enable the priest or deacon to know them a bit better.

- *Where do you work?*
  The couple usually feels at ease and is comfortable in conversing about the place and type of their employment. Doing so can prove interesting as well as informative for the interviewing clergyman. It likewise serves as an icebreaker in speaking with the engaged pair.

  Later, after the couple departs, it is good to make a few notes about this particular part of the discussion and insert them into the bride and groom's file. The data will seem fresh and indelible immediately following the interview, but those details will quickly slip from one's memory and need refreshment before the next appointment.

- *How did you meet?*
  This question leads the couple almost imperceptibly toward areas that are more personal and intimate. Some humor on the part of the priest or deacon about this topic can help them relax and be honest. More of these love matches begin at local bars than

at church picnics and it is helpful to acknowledge that reality in a lighthearted way.

- *Who was the first one to say, "I love you?"*
- *How did he propose?*
- *Why do you wish to marry him? Why her?*
- *What made you choose to be married in the Catholic Church?*
- *Why this particular church?*

That exchange will usually take only 20 minutes, but it breaks down barriers, establishes a connection and reassures the couple that they are welcomed to the parish.

Next in that initial session there follows a lengthy (about a half-hour) explanation of the practical marriage preparation details, often an appropriate video, and finally, completion of the FOCCUS (Facilitating Open Couple Communication, Understanding and Study) pre-marital inventory or instrument discussed in Chapter 8.

There is, of course, much more to follow in the preparatory process. However, I have found in working with those many engaged couples in the past decade that this process seems to work. They usually leave the office affirmed in their love and excited by what is to come. If their flame of faith was only flickering when they arrived, upon their departure it may be burning a bit more brightly.

CHAPTER SEVEN

SEVERAL BAPTISMAL CHALLENGES

The young public school teacher, married and mother of a two-year-old, was pregnant with their second child when her husband left for someone else. She was devastated by the abandonment.

After a successful delivery, she struggled mightily to cope, now as a single parent with two children under two.

Church on Sunday became a near impossibility for her in the first months after the birth.

Eventually she contacted her parish to arrange for the baptism.

A church representative refused her request because she wasn't attending Mass, declining even to discuss it until the beleaguered woman started to be there regularly for the Eucharist.

Official Guidance

Was the parish's response justified by Church regulations?

Participation at Sunday Mass clearly is a serious responsibility for Catholics. The *Catechism of the Catholic Church*, however, explicitly mentions the possibility of excusing causes: "Unless excused for a serious reason (for example, illness, the care

75

of infants) or dispensed by their own pastor" (Article 2181).

Moreover, on October 20, 1980, the Sacred Congregation for the Doctrine of the Faith issued an *Instruction on Infant Baptism* dealing with some of the practices and problems connected with infant baptism since the Second Vatican Council.

It initially provided "two great principles, the second of which is subordinate to the first."

1. Baptism, which is necessary for salvation, is the sign and the means of God's prevenient love, which frees us from original sin and communicates to us a share in divine life. Considered in itself, the gift of these blessings to infants must not be delayed.

2. Assurances must be given that the gift thus granted can grow by an authentic education in the faith and Christian life, in order to fulfill the true meaning of the sacrament. As a rule, these assurances are to be given by the parents or close relatives, although various substitutions are possible within the Christian community. But if these assurances are not really serious there can be grounds for delaying the sacrament; and if they are certainly non-existent the sacrament should even be refused (No. 28).

The document, in No. 30, then also adds three rules to assist in responding to families who seek their child's baptism but possess little faith or are non-Christian families.

1. "In this case the pastor will endeavor by means of clear-sighted and understanding dialogue to arouse the parents' interest in the sacrament they are requesting and make them aware of the responsibility that they are assuming."

2. "In fact the Church can only accede to the desire of these parents if they give an assurance that, once the child is baptized, it will be given the benefit of the Christian up-

bringing required by the sacrament. The Church must have a well-founded hope that the baptism will bear fruit."

3. "With regard to the assurances, any pledge giving well-founded hope for the Christian upbringing of the children deserves to be considered as sufficient."

Finally, the Vatican text describes several action alternatives:

1. "If the assurances given — for example, the choice of godparents who will take sincere care of the child, or the support of the community of the faithful — are sufficient, the priest cannot refuse to celebrate the sacrament without delay, as in the case of children of Christian families."

2. "If on the other hand they are insufficient, it will be prudent to delay baptism. However the pastors should keep in contact with the parents so as to secure, if possible, the conditions required on their part for the celebration of the sacrament. If even this solution fails, it can be suggested, as a last recourse, that the child be enrolled in a catechumenate to be given when the child reaches school age."

3. "It must be clear that the refusal of baptism is not a means of exercising pressure. Nor can one speak of refusal, still less of discrimination, but rather of educational delay, according to individual cases, aimed at helping the family to grow in faith or to become more aware of its responsibilities."[1]

In view of the tenor or implications of those official documents, what do you think of the parish's refusal to baptize the baby simply because of her absence from Sunday Mass even though she contacted the church and sought this sacrament?

---

[1] Joseph M. Champlin, *The Marginal Catholic, op. cit.*, pp. 114-117.

Underage Sponsor

A young married mother, having given birth to a first child, connects with the parish and asks that her brother, age 14, be one of the sponsors.

The priest or deacon, wishing to be firm and to follow Church rules, rejects the request, stating that Canon Law requires sponsors to be 16 and confirmed. The new mother is disappointed, perhaps deeply troubled by the negative response.

A closer look at both current circumstances and Church legislation could open the way to a kinder and gentler solution.

➤ Canon Law (874:2) states that a sponsor needs to have completed the sixteenth year, but adds "unless a different age has been established by the diocesan bishop or it seems to the pastor or minister that an exception is to be made for a just cause." The "just cause" required is much easier to satisfy legally than a "grave or serious cause"; almost any good reason is sufficient.

➤ The Code (874:3) declares that a sponsor must be confirmed, having already received the sacrament of the Most Holy Eucharist, and leading a life in harmony with the faith and the role to be undertaken.

➤ The lad in question is presently in preparation for Confirmation and presumably will receive this sacrament in about two years. Moreover, in preparation for that sacred event, he participates at Mass regularly, attends the prescribed classes and engages in several service projects. In addition, he has made or will join with the other candidates for the two scheduled retreats.

➤ Throughout the United States, several dioceses, including Portland in Maine, Saginaw in Michigan and Tyler in Texas, celebrate Confirmation prior to First Communion.

If the fourteen year-old lived in any of those places, he would have fulfilled that requirement of Canon 874:3.[2]

Considering all those elements, would not the spirit of the law allow the young man to become a sponsor for the baptism, understanding that in several years he would perfectly fulfill all of the requirements?

Other Special Requests

The clergy and pastoral ministers in parishes with a considerable number of baptisms rather frequently receive special requests involving sponsors or godparents.

Parents may ask for two of the same sex, or a baptized Christian who is not a Catholic, or one who is not baptized at all, or a non-believing individual, or a divorced and non-practicing Catholic, or more than two godparents.

This is not an exhaustive list of situations! The reasons for these special requests are many and often not expressed unless the clergy or pastoral minister seeks an explanation. For example, the non-Catholic parent wishes to invite a close non-Catholic relative for the task. Another illustration: one parent asks that an uncle, divorced and remarried out of the Church, but who has been very helpful to the parents in difficult situations, serve as a sponsor.

The requests usually are made with well-meaning, but earnest and intense emotions. The clergy and pastoral ministers are placed in an awkward position as they try to follow Church regulations, but at the same time to accommodate, if possible, desires of the parents.

---

[2] I treated this question of Underage Sponsor and also the subsequent issue of Same Sex Parents in summary fashion as a column "Liturgy and Life" in *The Priest* magazine for October 2006.

A few excerpts from the *Code of Canon Law* may be helpful in addressing these challenges.

"Insofar as possible one to be baptized is to be given a sponsor who is... together with the parents, to present an infant at the baptism, and who will help the baptized to lead a Christian life in harmony with baptism, and to fulfill faithfully the obligations connected with it" (Canon 872).

"Only one male or female sponsor or one of each is to be employed" (Canon 873).

In summary, there *must* be at least one sponsor, but there may be two, a male and a female sponsor. One sponsor is necessary; two sponsors are an option.

Pastoral ministers around the country using the "one must, but two may" Church regulation have resolved those kind of special requests in a variety of creative ways.

How would you respond to them?

Same Sex Parents

As archbishop of San Francisco, William Levada permitted gay couples to adopt "difficult to place" children through his Catholic Charities agency.

Later, however, succeeding Cardinal Ratzinger as head of the Congregation for the Doctrine of the Faith, he tightened up this approach. Writing to the archbishops of Boston and San Francisco, Cardinal Levada directed them to stop placing children for adoption with gay couples. His action was based on a document issued in 2003 by the same office under Cardinal Ratzinger. In addition, he mentioned a concern about "the potential scandal for the faithful should an archdiocese agency act contrary to the clear teachings of the Church's magisterium."[3]

---

[3] David Gibson, *The Rule of Benedict*, p. 318.

With that decision in mind, what should be done in this following case?

Female partners, both professional people, prayerful Catholics and Mass regulars, adopt through a secular agency an infant abandoned at a local hospital. They seek to have the baby baptized, both wishing and promising to raise the child as a Catholic.

The Church's official guidelines for baptism provide help here.

The previously cited 1980 Congregation for the Doctrine of the Faith *Instruction on Infant Baptism* includes a section: "Dialogue between pastors and families with little faith or non-Christian families," which states:

> It sometimes happens that pastors are approached by parents who have little faith and practice their religion only occasionally, or even by non-Christian parents who request baptism for their children for reasons that deserve consideration (No. 30).

In summary, the text, as we noted in detail earlier, offers these principles for guidance:

➤ The gift and gifts of baptism, necessary for salvation, considered as blessings in themselves, must not be delayed to infants.

➤ Assurances must be given that the gifts granted can grow by an authentic education in the faith and Christian life.

➤ The pastor or his delegate should engage in a clear sighted dialogue with the parents about the proposed baptism.

➤ There must be a well-founded hope, a *spes fundata,* that the baptism will bear fruit.

➤ "Any pledge giving a well-founded hope for the Christian

upbringing of the children deserves to be considered as sufficient" (No. 31).

Official Church rules thus allow the baptism of children whose parents have little faith, practice their religion only occasionally, or are not even Christians, but who give proper assurances that they will raise the youngsters Roman Catholic.

If that is the case, does it not seem that one might baptize the adopted child of these Catholic women in a same sex relationship who agree to raise the infant Roman Catholic?

The United States Conference of Catholic Bishops, in its November, 2006 statement, *Ministry to Persons with a Homosexual Inclination: Guidelines for Pastoral Care*, deals explicitly with that challenge.[4] The Bishops state that indeed one might baptize such children. Their words of guidance:

> Baptism of children in the case of same-sex couples presents a serious pastoral concern. Nevertheless, the Church does not refuse the Sacrament of Baptism to these children, but there must be a well-founded hope that the children will be brought up in the Catholic religion. In those cases where Baptism is permitted, pastoral ministers should exercise prudential judgment when preparing baptismal ceremonies. Also, in preparing the baptismal record, a distinction should be made between natural parents and adoptive parents.

---

[4]   United States Conference of Catholic Bishops, *Ministry to Persons with a Homosexual Inclination: Guidelines for Pastoral Care* (Washington, DC: USCCB Publishing, December, 2006), p. 20.

CHAPTER EIGHT

TO MARRY OR NOT TO MARRY

In their early courtship days when John and Christine went out for dinner, she regularly would reach over with her fork and take a portion of his entrée.

Having grown up with four brothers and forced to fight for his food, John resented her action. However, he repressed his anger. Instead, he reacted in passive-aggressive fashion by barricading his plate with water glasses, a bottle of wine or the salt and pepper shakers. That did not dissuade Christine; she simply moved through or around the obstacles.

Months later, in a weak moment, John somewhat exploded, abruptly asking her to stop. She immediately grew silent and said little for the rest of the evening. He knew that he had hurt her.

However, they had not yet learned to surface and resolve those delicate and difficult differences in their relationship. Nothing further was said and a minor, but still painful distance remained between them.

Several weeks later on a business trip, John sat in a restaurant and observed with interest an elderly couple near him. Sure enough, when their main courses arrived, the wife reached with a fork to sample her spouse's dinner. But the husband, unlike John, lifted his plate and extended it toward her.

That gesture struck home to John. He said to himself,

"That is what Christine was doing and telling me. It is all about sharing."

The priest who was to preside over this wedding invited John and Christine to write their hopes and expectations for the future, to do them separately without showing their words to each other, and present them to the priest at the rehearsal. He, in turn, with their permission, would use these two compositions as part of the homily.

John, just prior to the ceremony, thought about the older couple having dinner, about the great things Christine had already done for him, and how much he missed her eating off his plate. That reflection, he said, gave him hope. Somewhat of a poet, John, after retelling this incident, added these words for his hopes and expectations:

> I hoped that Chris would be eating from my plate the next time I was with her.
>
> I hoped that Chris would be eating from my plate the night I asked her to marry me.
>
> I hoped that Chris would be eating from my plate when we sat down to discuss our wedding plans.
>
> I hoped that Chris would be eating from my plate the evening of our first anniversary, and on the evenings of our second, twenty-fifth and fiftieth anniversaries.
>
> I hoped that Chris would be eating from my plate the evening she tells me we are having a baby.
>
> I hoped that Chris would be eating from my plate the evening we have dinner for our parents in our first house.
>
> I hoped that Chris would be eating from my plate when she feels sad or low.
>
> I hoped that Chris would be eating from my plate the evenings that I tell her how much I love her and need her.

I hope that Chris will be eating from my plate for years to come — because this will mean that we are together.

I thank God every day for giving me a life with Christine. She has shown me true love. Chris is my miracle.[1]

This touching story with its concluding "hopes and expectations" exemplifies the kind of faith-filled and solidly mature couples which bring great joy and pleasure to the clergy working with them. However, many seem not to possess that degree of faith or maturity.

Trying to Decide

One of the tensions which prompt pastoral ministers to prefer ten funerals to a single wedding is deciding whether or not to marry such particularly "marginal" couples. Their "marginal" nature may be spiritual — they seldom are at church and seem to possess little or no awareness of marriage as a sacrament. Or the "marginal" characteristics may be natural — they seem very immature or are rushing into the wedding or their relationship appears shaky at best.

May I make three suggestions which could prove helpful to the clergy and ministers in resolving this tension and relieving their anxiety?

1. *The words of Pope John Paul II*: In a 1981 apostolic exhortation, *The Christian Family in the Modern World*, the Holy Father provided some principles for dealing with the engaged who wish to marry in the Church, but whose faith and religious practice are questionable. Those principles,

---

[1] Joseph Champlin, *From the Heart* (Notre Dame, IN: Ave Maria Press, 1998), pp. 14-15.

incidentally, ran counter to then current pastoral practice in some areas of this country:

➤ The faith of the person(s) seeking marriage in the Church can exist in varying degrees. It is in the primary duty of pastors to facilitate a rediscovery, nourishing and maturing of this faith.

➤ The Church, however, also admits to the celebration of marriage those who are imperfectly disposed.

➤ A couple who decide to marry according to the divine plan, that is, to commit their whole lives in unbreakable love and unconditional faithfulness by an irrevocable nuptial consent, are reflecting, even if not in a fully conscious way, an attitude of profound obedience to God's will, an attitude which cannot exist without God's grace.

➤ With such a decision or consent, the couple has entered upon a journey toward salvation, a journey which with their upright intention and through the immediate preparation and celebration of the sacrament can be complemented and brought to completion.

➤ The fact that couples often request marriage in the Church for social rather than genuinely religious reasons is understandable. However, the fact that motives of a social nature are present is not enough to justify refusal by the pastor to celebrate the marriage.

➤ Engaged couples, by baptism, already share in Christ's marriage covenant with the Church. Moreover, by their right intention, described above, they have accepted God's plan for marriage. Therefore, given these two points, they at least implicitly consent to what the Church intends to do when she celebrates marriage.

➤ Insisting on further criteria that concern the faith level of the couple as a requirement for admission to the Church celebration of marriage involves great risks. It leads to the danger of making unfounded and discriminatory judgments, as well as to the peril of causing doubts about the validity of marriages already celebrated.

➤ Nevertheless, when engaged couples explicitly and formally reject what the Church intends to do in the marriage of baptized persons, the pastor cannot admit them to the celebration of the sacrament.

➤ The pastor is such circumstances must indicate to the couple his reluctance to defer the marriage and to stress that they, not the Church, are placing obstacles to such a celebration.[2]

Do these principles, especially the risk of insisting on further criteria, not provide a context for responding to questions like Mass attendance or registration in a parish?

2. *The Code of Canon Law.* One canon proposes a sacramental ideal, the reception of Confirmation, Penance and Eucharist before matrimony (Canon 1065:1, 2).

If they can do so without serious inconvenience, Catholics who have not yet received the sacrament of Confirmation are to receive it before being admitted to marriage.

It is strongly recommended that those to be married approach the sacraments of Penance and the Most Holy Eucharist so that they may fruitfully receive the sacrament of marriage.

That text would seem to indicate a distinction between marriage and those other sacraments.

Confirmation clearly is not necessary for the validity of

---

[2]   Joseph M. Champlin, *The Marginal Catholic, op. cit.*, pp. 149-153.

marriage. Catholics are encouraged to receive Confirmation if they can do so "without serious inconvenience." However, it is not essential for the reception of marriage.

Since matrimony is a sacrament of the living and requires the state of grace for full fruitfulness, the Code "strongly recommends" that couples approach the sacraments of Penance and Holy Eucharist prior to marriage.

However, it seems to imply that those two sacraments, while highly desirable, are not prerequisites for the marriage's validity.

3. *The impossibility of predicting the future.* A priest psychologist does extensive testing of applicants for the seminary and for the religious life; he also serves as a consultant for the diocesan marriage tribunal. This clergyman states quite frankly that he cannot predict the successful future of clients, but he can predict with moral certitude, their forthcoming failures.

The author of a premarital discussion instrument which helps couples recognize areas of agreement and disagreement, nevertheless maintains that it cannot evaluate the possibility of a couple's successful marriage, because it is not possible to measure future potential.

Pastoral ministers can give countless testimonies of surprises, of marriages "made in heaven" that did not work, and, on the other hand, dubious couplings of people who are presently preparing for their golden anniversaries. Those surprises extend to the preparation procedures as well. Most clergy could name couples who completed conscientiously and enthusiastically all the suggested steps to prepare for marriage, yet who separated before a decade passed. Conversely, they could name couples whose participation in the marital preparation was reluctant and spotty, but whose subsequent marriages have been strong and steady.

In addition to these observations, there is the ever present influence of divine grace which can change hearts, lead to a conversion of attitudes, and perhaps even turn a couple heading for marital disaster on to a different course leading to a successful relationship.

Preparing and Celebrating the Rite

In preparing for and celebrating the marriage ritual, a few pastoral suggestions may prove helpful.

◆ *Immediate introduction to the liturgy.* As we have mentioned, their wedding is for most couples the first major social event for which they are responsible. The church ceremony, of course, is a very significant part of this experience. Introducing the engaged pair to some of the liturgical possibilities at the initial interview often immediately elicits a very positive response from them.

A pastor from Virginia, after outlining the many alternative prayers, readings and blessings in the ritual, encourages them right from the start to make the process for selecting readings a means of fostering their communication skills and developing an ability to pray together.

He invites them to read in alternating fashion all 32 of the suggested biblical texts and their commentaries, narrowing them down to half dozen. Next, he suggests that they find a quiet spot, place themselves in a prayerful mood, then read and reflect on each of the preferred texts. As they do so, they can ask themselves what word, phrase or idea in the selection speaks to them in a

special way. Eventually, the couple chooses three for the liturgy
and notes them on the selection form.

◆ *Wedding musical showcase.* The Syracuse Cathedral's very
talented, professional and flexible director of music has
served at that position for three decades. He enjoys the
availability of a century-old 3,000 pipe organ, an impres-
sive grand Bosendorfer piano and a spacious structure with
marvelous acoustics. Given the traditional nature of the
church, its beautiful, ancient stained glass windows, and a
lengthy aisle, it is not surprising that some 75 couples annually select the Cathedral for their nuptials.

To provide these bridal parties and their families with an
experience of excellent and suitable music for their church service, the director hosts a Wedding Musical Showcase from 2:00-
4:00 p.m. on a Sunday in the fall and the spring. He assembles
a group of local musical artists — instrumentalists and vocalists
— to provide brief samples of what they could offer for the liturgy
itself as well as for the reception. They hear during that session
very fine cantors as well as a string quartet, bagpipes, harp and
flute, trumpet and, of course, organ and piano.

It, as it were, raises the musical bar and gives the engaged
a rich variety of options from which to choose.

◆ *Pre-marital inventories*: These instruments like FOCCUS
(Facilitating Open Couple Communication, Understanding
and Study) are not tests — although the engaged couple per-
sist in asking "How did we do on the tests?" They, rather, are
intended to serve as communication skill builders. I arrange
for the couple to complete the multi-question document at
the end of the first visit, a task requiring about a half-hour,
but which seems to generate interest and excitement between
the bride and groom.

One couple completing FOCCUS realized that she is a quick decision maker and he, a ponderer. Since the major expenses in a marriage seem to be a car, house and children's college education, it would be curious to observe how the purchase process plays out for them in their married life.

Another couple, older and secure job wise, realized that they never had discussed finances. Surveys indicate that the main challenges over the first five years of marriage are sex, time and money. Their FOCCUS experience helped them prepare for their fiscal discussions later on.

◆ *Pre-marital Investigation or Inquiry*: This document, administered under oath to the bride and groom individually, seeks the necessary legal information prior to the wedding, e.g., names, parents, sacramental background, freedom to marry, awareness of marital responsibilities.

In September, 1988 the NCCB approved a document, *Faithful to Each Other: A Catholic Handbook of Pastoral Help for Marriage Preparation,* which was published a year later by the United States Catholic Conference. Developed by several committees of bishops, it included a sample "Prenuptial Inquiry and Necessary Documentation." The form was designed to be more of a pastoral experience than a purely legal event. In the words of the handbook it hopefully "transforms what is often a mechanical, routine and legalistic burden into an encouraging, supportive and catechetical moment."[3]

The Handbook also suggests that the inquiry document *not* be done at the first meeting, but later, perhaps several months prior to the marriage itself.

---

[3] *Faithful to Each Other Forever: A Catholic Handbook of Pastoral Help for Marriage Preparation* (Washington, DC: United States Catholic Conference, 1989), p. 95. See also *Code of Canon Law,* c. 1063.

"There are sound pastoral reasons for completing the Prenuptial Inquiry Form after the couple have finished their marriage
preparation program and begun some of the planning for their
liturgy. Major obstacles or impediments will normally surface
during the first session with the Church representative and can be
addressed at that time. After their marriage preparation program
and the preliminary liturgy planning, the bride and groom will
usually be more comfortable and trusting with the Church representative. This creates a better climate for the inquiry experience
and offers a greater possibility that it will be a positive occasion for
them. Moreover, they will, through these formational and liturgical processes, generally have gained a deeper understanding of
the Church's teaching on marriage, reflected personally on their
own spiritual condition, and discussed some of the vital issues
surrounding the marriage (e.g., children, religious differences,
communication blocks). Such growth in those areas can make
their subsequent dialogue with the pastor or his delegate more
productive and satisfying."[4]

The form itself includes these questions: How would you
describe your practice of your religion? When did you last approach the sacrament of penance? When did you last receive
Holy Communion?[5]

I have found these three inquiries to be particularly insightful and informative.

The individual is usually puzzled by the first question about
the practice of religion. My clarification generally has been:
"Would you say that you go to Sunday Mass always, usually,
sometimes, rarely, or never?" Many, of course, respond "sometimes" or "rarely," but often I hear apologies about their neglect
and the intention to be more regular once married.

---

[4] *Ibid.*, p. 96.
[5] *Ibid.*, p. 101.

The second question frequently surfaces the fact that the last time for confession was in the far distant past, while the third question reveals that Holy Communion was not long ago.

I would then interrupt the process of completing the questionnaire with a few words like these:

> It would be a good idea to go to confession before you are married. You probably will be a bit uneasy about this but simply say to the priest: "Father, it has been a long time since I confessed, but I am getting married soon and would like to make a fresh start. Would you help me out?" There is another reason why it would be desirable to make a confession prior to the wedding. You both hope to have children. In about ten years or so, your youngster will be approaching First Penance and First Communion age. In most parishes today parents become the prime persons preparing a child for these sacraments. If you don't take care of this now, it will place you in an awkward position when that time comes to guide your little boy or girl to this sacrament of reconciliation. These booklets *Meeting the Merciful Christ* and *Why Go to Confession?* may help you with this challenge.[6] I think you will feel much better if you are able to do this before the wedding.

I have never checked back later to see how effective were these comments. But this brief intervention, hopefully soft, kind and gentle, was nevertheless, part of teaching, of being faithful, and of spiritually stretching the individuals.

---

[6] Joseph M. Champlin, *Why Go to Confession?* and *Meeting The Merciful Christ* (Cincinnati, Ohio: St. Anthony Messenger Press, 1996 and 1986, Revised Edition 2005).

◆ *Hopes and Expectations.* As a resident and then pastor in a suburban parish for fifteen years where there were over 50 marriages annually, I began to sense that many people, having attended several of these nuptial services, were familiar with my basic wedding homily. Now uneasy using those effective, but repeated concepts, I contemplated creating a half dozen new approaches during the quiet, wedding-wise, winter months. That never happened. Instead, the idea developed of inviting couples to compose their own hopes and expectations for the marriage and to follow the procedure described in the example which opened this chapter.

The results were remarkable. About 70% of couples took advantage of this invitation. I made copies of their hopes and expectations, returning the originals to them at the wedding itself, and now I possess a collection of over 700 quite diverse letters or hopes. Subsequent couples planning for their marriage have as part of their preparation process the opportunity to sample these letters or compositions as they originally were written.

Reading them during the homily adds a fresh, personal and unique element to the preacher's message as he seeks to blend the scripture selected and the lives — present and future — of this bride and groom. Ordinarily those words probably impact the family and guests more than the bridal pair. They, however, are encouraged at the ceremony itself to reread their own thoughts each year on their anniversaries.[7]

◆ *Rehearsals.* For reasons noted above, rehearsals pose a particular challenge for the clergy. When two or three are scheduled back-to-back on a given evening, there can be a significant drain on the leader's physical and emotional energy.

---

[7] Joseph M. Champlin, *From the Heart, op. cit.* This booklet describes in detail the process and contains around 10 actual samples of these hopes and expectations.

Nevertheless, rehearsal time is an additional teachable and touchable moment for the bride and groom who tend to be quite excited, but stressed and anxious to have everything go well and smoothly.

A veteran parish priest at the Cathedral served as a mentor for me during my first year after ordination. I clearly recall his words even today, a half-century later: "Be careful at rehearsals. If you are kind to people, they will never forget you; if not, they will never forgive you." I also vividly recall the words a handball partner spoke to me decades ago. A tremendous competitor and perfectionist not only on the court, but in every aspect of life, this Protestant man married a Catholic girl at her rural parish. Years after the wedding, he still spoke with deep bitterness about the priest. Why? At the rehearsal he, the groom, asked to run through the procession a second time, just to be sure about what to do. The priest refused. His resentment over that refusal apparently will last forever.

Developing a corps of six married couples as rehearsal co-ordinators wonderfully resolved many of those challenges. They worked out a schedule so that no one pair felt burdened; some would even conduct all three rehearsals on a particular night; they received a modest stipend for each rehearsal, although no one expected or demanded it; they often treated themselves to a dinner after the evening's task.

I still would meet the wedding party at the start of the rehearsal — securing the license, having it signed, checking the selection form with all their choices and variables, receiving hopes and expectations if they had written them, welcoming the entire group with a little humor, an explanation of the church building, and a biblical prayer, then introducing the rehearsal coordinators and disappearing from the scene.

Those coordinators eased the burden of arranging and per-forming 75 weddings each year, as did the competent secretaries

who completed the clerical tasks required before and after the
ceremony.

Annulments

During the initial interview the response to an informal and
routine question, "The first marriage for both of you?" enables
the clergyman to move on with the marriage preparation details
or stops the process in its tracks. If the answer is negative, then
we need to explore the often complex and frequently sensitive
circumstances of a previous marriage.

The following sample statement is rather blunt, but quite accurate: If there is a previous marriage, there needs to be a record of
the death of that spouse or a Catholic Church annulment before
there may be a second marriage in the Catholic Church.

Exploring and obtaining an annulment based upon the
"lack of form," i.e., the marriage of a baptized Catholic before
someone other than a Catholic clergyman is relatively simple. Exploring and obtaining an annulment where the previous marriage
of a baptized Catholic was witnessed by a Catholic clergyman
or where two non-Catholics were married is more complicated.

Explaining this requires a review of Jesus' teaching on
divorce and the Church's obligation to follow his words. While
the Church presumes all marriages to be binding and lifelong,
there is a process which examines a couple's relationship from the
very beginning to assure all the essential elements of marriage
are present. Lacking one or more of these elements, the Church
may declare the marriage null and void.

Working with partners of a broken marriage, I recommend
the following process to help them identify the missing element
or elements:

As you reflect upon the marriage, ask yourself: Was there something missing right from the start, something radically wrong from day one? Before the wedding, were there warning signals, red flags which you may have dismissed simply as the cold-feet anxieties rather common for couples prior to a nuptial service? Did you suffer deep difficulties early in your marital life and worry about them, but never being married before, judged they were merely the expected burdensome part of marriage? Now, perhaps years later, you view those before the marriage signals or early marriage difficulties as symptomatic of a much more serious problem, a radical malfunctioning in your relationship.

I have assisted dozens of these formal cases over the years since the new procedures were introduced in the United States some decades ago. The prospect may seem daunting at the start and delving into these past issues can be painful. Often, however, the process proves to be healing and therapeutic as well as opening the door to a future wedding in the Church.[8]

A troubled relatively young woman spoke with me early on in my priesthood. Her husband had just revealed that he was homosexual and had permanently left her. "What about my future?" she asked. Would she be allowed to marry again in the Church?

I gave her a dismal response based on the annulment procedures in the late 1950's — a long process, several years at best, very burdensome in details, sometimes requiring a reply from Rome, and with a positive outcome often quite doubtful.

---

[8] Joseph M. Champlin, "10 Questions About Annulment," *Catholic Update* (Cincinnati, OH: St. Anthony Messenger Press, 2002), No. C, 1002, p. 2.

She left in tears.

Those who long for a return to the glory days of the Church before the Second Vatican Council (many of whom never experienced that era) should be a bit cautious in their euphoric description of this period. That broken-hearted woman left in tears, without any hope, because of the procedures in place then. Today, with the process we now follow, she might have walked away with hope, an opportunity to be healed of her pain and a real possibility of marrying again in the Church.

CHAPTER NINE

BURYING THE DEAD

Susan's brother Bill, although he was afflicted with serious medical difficulties throughout life, died unexpectedly in his forties, alone and out of state. Because of the complications surrounding Bill's death, family members had a few extra days before the funeral to share their memories of him in large gatherings and small clusters.

That extended group communicated these diverse and rich recollections with Susan the day before the church service. She then sat down at the computer for a half-hour and prepared the words of remembrance, excerpts of which follow. Names have been changed for privacy purposes.

> Over the past month, our family gathered on several occasions. We celebrated a wedding and a 50th wedding anniversary. I'm sure we never thought that our next gathering would be here today, under these circumstances.
>
> Beloved Bill... friend, cousin, nephew, uncle, brother-in-law, son, you will forever be in our hearts.
>
> For someone dealing with so many struggles in life, Bill had a tremendous sense of humor, not to mention a positive outlook. Bill would preface so many things

by saying, "Don't worry" or "That's OK." Whenever you told him about something difficult you were dealing with, or how bad your day was, Bill would say, "Well, at least you have..." and he would fill in the blank.

His sense of humor is what drove everyone else crazy. My parents recall pulling up to their home after being away only to see a "For Sale" sign that Bill placed in the front yard. I am not sure whether or not they thought it was as funny as Bill did.

You could always count on Bill to answer the phone with "Joe's Bar and Grill" or "County Jail." He would often call me at work disguising his voice... "Hello, yes, I have a million dollars to invest and I hope you can help me." If you ever were out to eat with him and he had an older waitress, he would flatter her by calling her "Young lady" or "Teenager" over and over. He did anything he could to make everyone feel good, even those he barely knew. Bill put a smile on so many faces and his kindness will never be forgotten.

He was an avid sports fan and LOVED his Detroit Tigers. Bill and my parents spoke many times last week about the games the Tigers won. We can only hope that on Saturday, October 14th when the Tigers won the pennant that Bill somehow knew.

His love for animals was extraordinary to the point where he could approach any unfamiliar animal just to get close enough to show his affection. You can imagine how thrilled my parents were over this when Bill was a young child. We remember many dogs in cars with a cracked window baring their teeth. It amazed us how they instantly settled upon Bill's approach. He had a special connection.

Our golden retriever Brittany was Bill's very best friend. She loved Bill just as he loved her and everyone in his life... truly and unconditionally. You knew that wherever Bill was Brittany was also.

When Bill left this city you can imagine how difficult it was for Mom and Dad. They visited Bill often and he was so proud to show them around. It was hard for Bill to get home and when he did he only wanted to relax and spend time with family. Bill was elated when his niece and nephew arrived and he made special visits to meet them.

Though Bill wanted children of his own one day, he never let you know what he was hurting for or what his life was lacking; he was genuinely happy for others.

Growing up in a family with two sisters I am sure Bill went out of his mind quite often. We had some pretty good fights and if he were sitting here right now I am sure he would love me to elaborate. Bill felt so fortunate for his eventual brothers-in-law, John and Sam. They quickly established a strong bond of brotherly love.

More than anything, Bill loved to reminisce. He would have our parents tell stories over and over, especially the ones that would incriminate them. At family gatherings he would get everyone at the table telling stories from the past and we would all laugh until we cried.

Our family has heard from a lot of people this week. A few of the condolences really stand out. Tim, his cousin, told my mother, "I aspire to lead my life more like Bill. Everyone who knew Bill had something good to take from him. If everyone were a little more

like Bill, then the world would be a better place."
When my mother thanked him, Tim said, "Don't
thank me. Thank Bill."

Aunt Arlene said it best. "When Bill woke up he
was in the arms of the Lord and he will have no more
pain and suffering. He is in heaven with his Grandparents and Brittany."

They say love is the tie that binds. I believe this is
true and Bill is our common thread. For our family
that was here with us this week and for those of you
here with us today, you cannot imagine how much
your love and support has meant to our family. Bill
loved each and every one of you.

Bill, today you breathe new life into us through
your compassion for others and unconditional love.
These are the lessons we will take from you. If we
could have just one more minute with you to tell you
how much you meant, it would provide some comfort
rather than wondering whether or not we told you
enough. We hope you know how much we will always
love you and how much you will be missed. May God
bless you always.

Words of Remembrance

As is usually the case, when Susan read these prepared
remarks people wept and laughed, smiled and nodded in agreement, were intrigued by the details of his life and inspired by
Bill's good deeds, many of which were unknown to a majority
of those present.

When Susan finished her roughly ten minute Words of Remembrance, the pastor as presiding priest simply complimented
her with, "Well done."

The *Order of Christian Funerals* published in 1989, following the directives of the Second Vatican Council, explicitly urges active participation by the bereaved family in the preparation and celebration of the funeral service whether with or outside Mass. It also directs that "a brief homily based on the readings is always given after the gospel reading at the funeral liturgy and may also be given after the readings at the vigil service; but there is never to be a eulogy" (No. 27).[1]

This *Order of Christian Funerals* also introduced a new feature — Words of Remembrance similar to those prepared and spoken by Susan at her brother's service.

At the Vigil for the Deceased: "A member or a friend of the family may speak in remembrance of the deceased" (No. 80).

At the Funeral Mass: "A member or a friend of the family may speak in remembrance of the deceased before the final commendation begins" (No. 170).

At the Funeral Liturgy Outside Mass: "A member or a friend of the family may speak in remembrance of the deceased before the final commendation begins" (No. 197).

Similarly worded directives occur for three other situations in the *Order of Christian Funerals*: at the Vigil for a Deceased Child (No. 246); at the Funeral Mass for a Deceased Child (No. 288); at the Funeral Outside of Mass for a Deceased Child (No. 309).

These repeated rubrics about Words of Remembrance have been widely implemented throughout the United States, but with uneven results.

Priests and deacons frequently have patiently, but painfully endured Words of Remembrance which were given by several speakers rather than just one, were excessively long, and were sometimes inappropriate in content.

---

[1] *Order of Christian Funerals including Appendix 2: Cremation* (NJ: Catholic Book Publishing Co., 1998), No. 27.

In reaction to those bad experiences some leaders on the parish and diocesan levels have prohibited these Words of Remembrance or limited them to the Vigil Service. Others, recognizing their great pastoral value for the bereaved, have retained them, but required that there be only one speaker (as the rubric states) and that the remarks be written out beforehand.

The process which Susan's family followed and her own carefully prepared remarks illustrate how effective and appropriate the Words of Remembrance can be.

Cremation

Prior to 1997 three factors created tensions for pastoral ministers in connection with cremation.

First, the several centuries old church prohibition on cremation, a restriction imposed because the practice grew out of and reflected an absence of belief in the Resurrection. Many Catholics continue to think that prohibition is still in effect.

Secondly, the rapid contemporary increase in the number of cremations. Currently about one quarter of Americans select cremation and it is projected that the number will rise to a third by 2010.

Thirdly, the absence of approved liturgical rites for the Catholic burial of cremains.

That tension was, for the most part, eliminated in 1997 with the Vatican approval of an Appendix to the *U.S. Order of Christian Funerals* specifically dealing with cremation.

The text explicitly declared that the Church prefers burial of the body. Moreover, it stresses that pastors and catechists on all levels should explain and promote this preference.

The reasons given for that preference are many, of which these are most compelling: the example of Jesus whose body was laid in a tomb; the fact that these bodies were once washed in baptism, anointed with the oil of salvation, and fed with the Bread of Life; the long-held teaching that the body is a temple of the Holy Spirit and destined for future glory at the resurrection of the dead; a conviction that the presence of the body during calling hours and all the funeral rites helps mourners face the reality of a person's death.

Nevertheless, the Church now explicitly allows cremation and provides for a variety of rites to cover different situations which arise.

The Church prefers that the cremation take place after the funeral liturgy, but recognizes that circumstances sometimes dictate cremation preceding the funeral liturgy. It provides ritual directions and actual texts for both situations.[2]

Many funeral directors have developed a system which harmonizes the Church's ideal with the practical circumstances involving cremation. They offer the option of a rental casket with its replaceable interior. In this scenario, the body is available for the viewing or calling hours, transferred to the church for the service, and afterwards returned to the funeral home. There the interior container with the body is removed and transported to the crematory.

One funeral home which conducts over 150 services (with 20% involving cremation) each year estimates that about half of those involving cremation select this rental casket/replaceable interior procedure.

Those who wish to donate their organs or bodies after death enjoy the support of Church teachings. The *Catechism of the Catholic Church* terms this decision "a noble and meritorious act and is to be encouraged as an expression of generous solidarity" (Article 2296).

---

[2] *Ibid.,* Nos. 418-431.

However, those who express a wish that their entire body be donated to science or a medical school for use by students studying to become physicians encounter a unique situation. The body, in that context, is taken immediately upon death to the recipient institution, stored for future use, and after one or two years, cremated, with the remains if requested, returned to the next of kin.

That process would seem to suggest two services: a funeral Mass or service at the time of death with no body or ashes present and a Memorial Mass or service with the cremains a year or two later.

Such a procedure would be consistent with the Church's remarkably succinct summary of pastoral directives about the cremated remains.

> The cremated remains of a body should be treated with the same respect given to the human body from which they come. This includes the use of a worthy vessel to contain the ashes, the manner in which they are carried, the care and attention to appropriate placement and transport, and the final disposition. The cremated remains should be buried in a grave or entombed in a mausoleum or columbarium. The practice of scattering cremated remains on the sea, from the air, or on the ground, or keeping cremated remains in the home of a relative or friend of the deceased are not the reverent disposition that the Church requires. Whenever possible, appropriate means for recording with dignity the memory of the deceased should be adopted, such as a plaque or stone which records the name of the deceased.[3]

---

[3] *Ibid.*, No. 417.

Two parishes, located in the North Carolina foothills and within the Blue Ridge Mountains, St. William in Murphy and Immaculate Heart of Mary in Hayesville, have nicely implemented those directives.

Located in Baptist territory with only a 2% Roman Catholic population, both churches have created reflective areas near the church buildings, each of which contains a columbarium for the cremated remains of parishioners.

In one, several freestanding brick walls include small rectangular spaces for urns. A marble marker notes the name and appropriate dates of the deceased individual.

In the other, the burial is in the earth with similar markers flat on the ground likewise with name and dates.

Both parishes provide the urn, and the cost for a space is quite reasonable.

The nearness of each columbarium to the church makes committal services immediately after funeral Masses a rather easy and natural extension of the *Order of Christian Funerals.*[4]

Intercommunion

At a recent large funeral for a public person killed in tragic circumstances, the pastor and presiding priest made a pre-Communion announcement; his words echoed an advisory which another priest issues in similar circumstances:

> For those who are Roman Catholic and in the state of grace — meaning you are not in serious sin — you may now come forward for Holy Communion. For

---

[4] Joseph M. Champlin, "Being Catholic in Baptist Territory" a Liturgy and Life column for *The Priest*, April 2007.

those who are not Catholic, we are unable to offer you
the sacrament at this time. However, we do look forward to the day when the separation among Christians
will come to an end and we can once again be united
at the table of the Lord. For now, we encourage you
to make a spiritual communion, inviting the Lord to
be present in your heart.

A flurry of responses, both pro and con, soon appeared in
the local paper.

On one side, to illustrate, a writer sharply criticized the pastor and his announcement, arguing that Jesus welcomed everyone
and we should follow his example, allowing all present at funerals
to receive Communion.

On the other side, again as an example, a priest corre-
spondent vehemently maintained that out of respect for the
sacrament only Roman Catholics are allowed to receive the
Eucharist.

Official Church legislation on this matter could make cor-
respondents on both sides uncomfortable: those who maintain
"everyone is welcome" and others who stress that only Roman
Catholics may receive the Eucharist.

Canon 844:

No. 3: Catholic ministers may licitly administer the
sacraments of penance, Eucharist and anointing of the
sick to members of the oriental churches which do not
have full communion with the Catholic Church, if
they ask on their own for the sacraments and are properly disposed. This holds also for members of other
churches, which in the judgment of the Apostolic See
are in the same condition as the oriental churches as
far as these sacraments are concerned.

No. 4: If the danger of death is present or other grave necessity, in the judgment of the diocesan bishop or the conference of bishops, Catholic ministers may licitly administer these sacraments to other Christians who do not have full communion with the Catholic Church, who cannot approach a minister of their own community and on their own ask for it, provided they manifest Catholic faith in these sacraments and are properly disposed.

The Code also cautions that neither the diocesan bishop nor the conference of bishops is to enact general norms without consulting at least the local competent authority of the interested non-Catholic church or community.

A Practical Example

Here is an example and application of No. 4.

An Episcopal wife and her Roman Catholic husband lived in a sparsely settled section of the mid-west. Both were faith-filled persons and regular churchgoers. However, the nearest Episcopal parish was over a hundred miles away; the Roman Catholic parish but a short distance down the road.

Approaching her own minister or Episcopal priest on a regular basis was a moral impossibility, making this a grave spiritual necessity for the woman. She was anxious to receive and on her own asked for Holy Communion at the Sunday Eucharist. According to the Code, she appeared to fulfill the necessary conditions and should be allowed to receive not only the Holy Eucharist, but Penance and Anointing of the Sick as well.

She in fact did participate every Sunday in Holy Communion at the local Catholic church and occasionally made the long journey to her Episcopal parish for the sacraments.

A few dioceses in the past have extended the "grave necessity" circumstance to include individuals, but not groups, for
occasions like First Communions, Marriages and Funerals. But
the same conditions apply: they must be baptized Christians, ask
for the sacrament on their own and manifest a Catholic faith in
the Eucharist.[5]

In 1996, the United States Catholic Conference issued
"Guidelines for the Reception of Communion" which are now
published in missalettes used for Eucharistic worship.

Addressing "Fellow Christians," the guidelines include these
two sentences:

> Because Catholics believe that celebration of the Eu-
> charist is a sign of the reality of the oneness of faith, life
> and worship, members of those churches with whom
> we are not fully united are ordinarily not admitted to
> Holy Communion. Eucharistic sharing in exceptional
> circumstances by other Christians requires permission
> according to the directives of the diocesan bishop and
> by the provisions of Canon Law (Canon 844 #4).

The term "ordinarily" and the phrase "in exceptional circumstances" reflect those flexible directives of the *Code of Canon
Law* cited above.

I have been present for funerals at which the presiding
priest has made a statement prior to Communion similar to the
one at the beginning of this section, or has issued a more generic
invitation for all who believe in Christ and in the Eucharist to
receive Communion, or simply remained silent about this particular issue.

---

[5]   Joseph M. Champlin, "Intercommunion" for a Liturgy and Life column in *The Priest*,
January 2007.

Odds and Ends

Many, probably most parishes have pastoral ministers who specialize in funeral preparation or *bereavement committees* serving in a similar capacity.

They assist the families in selecting the readings, prayers and blessings, actively engage them and others in the ceremony itself, develop a program for the service, coordinate a luncheon for the family and others afterwards, then follow through with support for the bereaved in the months following the funeral.

That individual or committee also can provide the priest or deacon with personal information about the deceased and the bereaved family as he prepares the homily.

The *funeral homily* is, as noted, not to be a eulogy. However, there needs to be a real connection between the biblical texts, the funeral ritual and the person being buried. While details about the life of the deceased will surely surface in the Words of Remembrance, the preacher must still give the homily an individualized or personal character. Without that touch, the liturgy will not impact those present as it can and should.

Funerals choirs: A small, but very dedicated group of persons, who generously sing at every funeral, have become quite common in the United States. They add to the beauty of the occasion and facilitate congregational participation.

Music

With churches which have ambitious musical programs, it is possible to embellish the funeral liturgy with a family's personal requests. That can become a delicate issue, however, when the bereaved sometimes ask for inappropriate songs or melodies.

Any discussion of contemporary Catholic Church music directives probably should begin with the 1903 *Motu proprio* of Pope Pius X which encouraged active participation by the faithful in song, especially through the restoration of Gregorian Chant.

It would continue with the Encyclical Letter of Pope Pius XII in 1955 on Sacred Music. He said that the dignity and lofty purpose of sacred music consists, among other benefits, in "its special power and excellence to lift up to God the minds of the faithful who are present."

A decade later in the *Constitution on the Sacred Liturgy* the bishops stated: "Religious singing by the people is to be skillfully fostered, so that in devotions and sacred exercises, as also during liturgical services, the voices of the faithful may ring out."[6]

More to the point on this discussion are paragraphs 30-31 in the General Introduction for the *Order of Christian Funerals*:

> Music is integral to the funeral rites. It allows the community to express convictions and feelings that words alone may fail to convey. It has the power to console and uplift mourners and to strengthen the unity of the assembly in faith and love.
>
> The texts of the songs chosen for a particular celebration should express the paschal mystery of the Lord's suffering, death, and triumph over death and should be related to the readings from Scripture.
>
> Since music can evoke strong feelings, the music for the celebration of the funeral rites should be chosen with great care. The music at funerals should support, console, and uplift the participants and should help to

---

[6]   P. Kevin Seasoltz, *The New Liturgy: A Documentation 1903-1965* (Collegeville, MN: The Liturgical Press, 1966), pp. 3-10, 107-159, particularly No. 31; pp. 473-500, particularly No. 118.

create in them a spirit of hope in Christ's victory over death and in the Christian's share in that victory.[7]

What kind of music is then appropriate for worship?

It should be artistically excellent or good and orthodox in language; it should engage the hearts and even the lips of participants; it also should be appropriate for the entire service and fit the function of the rite at which it occurs.

The most popular request for music at Catholic funerals is very likely a solo rendition of "Danny Boy" — usually after Communion and prior to the Rite of Commendation. How well, or poorly, does "Danny Boy" fulfill those four requirements for suitable music at worship?

> *Artistically excellent or good*: "Danny Boy" has a legendary history dating back to the 1600's. Rory Dale O'Cahan, a blind harpist and member of the clan which had suffered two cruel injustices, composed this haunting tune of pain and passion. It came to be called "The O'Cahan Lament."

Jane Ross lived in the early 1800's and was a private music teacher and interested in Irish airs. One day in 1851, she heard Blind Jimmy, a blind itinerant street fiddler play this air or tune of "unequalled beauty." Struck by it, she asked him to play it again as she jotted down the notations of the tune. Ms. Ross had never heard the melody before and Blind Jimmy could not recall its history.

Subsequently, she sent it to Dublin to George Petrie who also was a collector of Irish airs. She added a comment that it was "very old and the composer unknown," yet both agreed that it was a piece of "considerable melodic beauty."

---

[7] *Order of Christian Funerals, op., cit.*, Nos. 30-31.

Petrie in 1855 published this unknown Irish lament as part of his famous collection.

Since Ross was from the county of Londonderry, he called that particular piece "The Londonderry Air."

There were attempts, all unsuccessful, to compose lyrics for this air. People simply had to whistle, hum or play it without words. Then in 1910, Fred Weatherley, living in Colorado, experienced the worst years of his life. The threat of a possible war and the death of his son and father within three months of each other devastated the man. Those experiences prompted him to write a set of lyrics which summed up both the pain of his loss and also the beauty of hope. He longed for the day he could link these words with a melody of equal passion.

Two years later, having never before heard "The Londonderry Air," he played the tune on the piano for the first time and softly sang his words to the melody. It was as if they had been created together. Only a few adjustments were necessary to match his lyrics with the melody. "Danny Boy" emerged from this, called by some "the most beautiful love song in the world."[8]

The sheet music for "Danny Boy" notes: "Words by Fred Weatherley" "Music from an old Irish Air."

The song, then, has certainly passed the test of time, enjoys a remarkable history and been termed a melody of "considerable melodic beauty." Would today's trained musicians term it a piece that is artistically excellent or good?

> *Orthodox in language.* The lyrics are not explicitly religious in a Catholic sense.

They do not mention God, the Trinity, Jesus or the Church. But the words express love, loss and hope, deeply spiritual sen-

---

8   *The Legend of Danny Boy* (Bangor, Co. Down, Northern Ireland: The Danny Boy Trading Co., Ltd, 1995). I am indebted to Rosemary Carr for lending me this fascinating little book together with a tape of the song.

timents and attitudes of the mind and heart reflected in the worship traditions of Catholicism and other Christian denominations. Moreover, the lyrics contain nothing inappropriate or irreverent.

> *Engage the hearts and lips of participants.* People as a group do not usually sing "Danny Boy." A talented artist generally solos the piece. But do those themes of love and hope touch the hearts of listeners? That haunting melody grew out of great pain and suffering: the exploitation of one's private property and life imprisonment without trial, centuries of violent conflicts, departures to America during the Potato Famine as well as all the personal and family losses that occur in a lifetime.

Those at a funeral may not be aware of that history with its love, loss and hope. But the words and melody expressing these sentiments surely move them deeply, touching as only music can, similar painful sorrows and deep yearnings for eventual reunions.

> *Appropriate for entire service and fits the function of the rite at which it occurs.*

"Danny Boy" at funerals, as noted before most frequently occurs after Communion and before the Final Commendation. The *General Instruction of the Roman Missal* in two places directs that after Communion the priest and faithful spend some time praying privately. Furthermore, it suggests: "A sacred silence may now be observed for some period of time, or a Psalm or another canticle of praise or a hymn may be sung."[9]

---

[9]   *General Instruction of the Roman Missal* (Washington, DC: United States Conference of Catholic Bishops, 2003), Nos. 88 and 164.

As we have seen, the Funeral Mass or Funeral Without a Mass, seeks to express solidarity with the bereaved, link their pain with the Paschal Mystery of Christ and express their hopes for resurrection and eventual reunion.

"Danny Boy"'s haunting melody and words convey that same message, especially in its final phrases:

> But when ye come and all the flowers are dying.
>   If I am dead, as dead I well may be.
> Ye'll come and find the place where I am lying.
>   And kneel and say an Ave there for me.
> And I shall hear, though soft you tread above me.
>   And my grave will warmer, sweeter be,
> For you will bend and tell me that you love me,
>   And I shall sleep in peace, until you come to me![10]

Does "Danny Boy" meet those requirements for suitable music at worship? Is the desire for it as described a reasonable and appropriate request?

Here a firmness, yet flexibility, is in order, sometimes bending a bit because of the highly emotional climate which surrounds burying the dead.

---

[10] *The Legend of Danny Boy, op. cit.*, p. 1.

CHAPTER TEN

SEEKING A BALANCE

Saint Benedict the monk (480-550) was of a distinguished family in Nursia, now part of Italy, and later studied in Rome. At
about 20 years of age he became troubled by the world in which
he lived — the corrupt morals of his fellow students, pagan armies
on the march, the Church torn by schism and the great suffering
of people caused by war.

He abandoned studies, gave up his inheritance and became a
hermit, quite withdrawn from the world. For three years he lived
an isolated life in a cave high up in the mountains at Subiacco.
Eventually some were attracted by his holiness and sought him
to be leader of a local monastery. That venture failed, but later
he was urged to found several monasteries, each with a presiding abbot. Eventually he established the famous monastery at
Monte Cassino commanding three valleys which ran toward
that mountain.

It was there that he composed his Rule which became the
foundation text for western monasticism and the beginnings of
the Benedictine Order.

The Rule of Benedict proposes in many instances balance as
the key to peace, holiness and happiness. The abbot, he taught,
"Must be stern, yet kind and flexible, adapting his methods to

the needs of each monk and the good of all."[1]

A number of St. Benedict's pithy sayings reflect that goal of balance.

"Put Christ before all else." "Prefer nothing to the love of God." Be faithful to Christ, his teaching and his call at all times and all costs.

Ora et Labora: "Pray and work." The Benedictine style of life balances manual work, public prayer, personal reflection and service to the poor of the community.

Ubi hospes venit, ibi Christus venit: "Whenever a guest comes, Christ comes." Despite a desire to withdraw from the world, the arrival of any guests demands a swift and loving response.

Nihil nimis: "Nothing excessive." Those two words capture in essence Benedict's approach to work and prayer, eating and sleeping, individual solitude and community relationships.

We celebrate the feast of St. Benedict on July 10.

It has been said that the Benedictine success is due largely to the Rule's "underlying balance, moderation and humanity."[2]

Pope Benedict XVI

We would naturally expect Pope Benedict XVI to emulate the teachings and example of that saint whose name he chose.

As we noted at the beginning of this book, on his first anniversary as the Roman Pontiff he expressed his desire to be a "firm, but gentle shepherd." "Firm" and "faithful" are closely related terms; "gentle" is also very near to "kind" and "flexible."

---

[1] Robert Ellsberg, *All Saints* (New York: Crossroad Publishing Company, 1998), pp. 297-298. For this material on St. Benedict also see Leonard Foley, O.F.M. and Pat McCloskey, O.F.M., *Saint of the Day* (Cincinnati, OH: St. Anthony Messenger Press, 2001), pp. 150-151 and Enzo Lodi, *Saints of the Roman Calendar* (New York: Alba House, 1992), pp. 178-180.

[2] *Ibid.*, Ellsberg, p. 298.

His early actions as the Holy Father revealed that firmness to Christ and his teachings.

➤ On September 4-5, 2006, more than 150 representatives of world religions gathered in Assisi to celebrate the twentieth anniversary of an epochal first inter-religious day of prayer for peace held there and prompted by Pope John Paul II. Bishop William Murphy, now of Rockville Centre, was at that time Undersecretary of the Pontifical Commission for Justice and Peace and helped arrange this event. In a fascinating article for *America*, he described the genesis of that remarkable gathering and the extreme delicateness of the preparation efforts.[3]

Pope Benedict sent a message to Assisi for that 20th anniversary gathering. After praising the initial event and this replication of it, the Holy Father cautioned that as then, twenty years ago, and so now, such an inter-religious prayer meeting should not "lend itself to syncretist interpretations founded on a relativistic concept."

He went on to say that "the conveyance of differences must not convey an impression of surrendering to that relativism that decries the meaning of truth itself and the possibility of attaining it."[4]

➤ On June 9, 2006, the Holy Father responded negatively to a request from the United States Conference of Catholic Bishops for an extension of an indult permitting extraordinary ministers to assist with the purification of sacred vessels at Mass. He did so through Cardinal Francis Arinze, Prefect

---

[3] Most Rev. William F. Murphy, "Remembering Assisi After 20 Years," *America*, October 23, 2006, pp. 10-13.

[4] *Origins*, Volume 36, Number 17, October 5, 2006, pp. 263-266.

of the Congregation for Divine Worship and the Discipline of the Sacraments.[5] This decision meant he had rejected a request of the U.S. Bishops, reversed an already established liturgical practice in this country and affected the lives of probably several hundred thousand extraordinary ministers of Holy Communion throughout the nation.

Both those actions represented a definite firmness of approach. However, other incidents reflected the style of a gentle shepherd.

➤ In his epochal November 2006 visit to Turkey, Pope Benedict XVI joined the Orthodox Ecumenical Patriarch Bartholomew of Constantinople in a unique prayer service at Istanbul's Orthodox Church of Saint George. They both lit votive candles, walked up the center aisle to generous applause, with their path clouded by incense. A choir chanted antiphons commemorating St. Peter and St. Paul, the patron saints of Rome, and St. Andrew, the patron of the Patriarchal See of Constantinople (now called Istanbul). They listened to a reading from the prophet Zechariah, calling the peoples of East and West to assemble again in Jerusalem. After praying the Our Father, each talked, both speaking of their shared heritage and the need to heal divisions.[6]

➤ During that same visit, the Holy Father on November 30 joined Mustafa Cagrici, the grand mufti of Istanbul, in silent prayer facing Mecca at the Blue Mosque in Istanbul. It was only the second time that any pope had entered a mosque.[7]

---

[5] *Newsletter*, Committee on the Liturgy, Volume XLII, October 2006, pp. 37-40.

[6] *Crux of the News*, December 4, 2006, p. 1.

[7] *National Catholic Reporter*, December 15, 2006, p. 7.

The picture of the event, instantly communicated throughout the world, may indeed have extended as powerful impact as
did the photo of Pope John Paul II in a Roman prison sitting
across from his convicted assailant and holding the man's hands
in reconciliation.

The editors of *Commonweal* reflected upon the meaning
and value of this papal pilgrimage to Turkey:

Pope Benedict XVI returned to Rome from Turkey
last month a virtual conqueror. He had achieved the
improbable during his four-day visit: substantive steps
toward political, cultural, and religious rapprochement
with the east. The pope had pleased his Turkish hosts
by indicating a positive attitude toward Turkey's eventual admission to the European Union (EU). He then
managed to reassure aggrieved Turkish Muslims of his
respect for their faith and their religious and cultural
achievements — this barely two months after his ill-
conceived remarks at Regensburg had sparked violent
demonstrations across the Muslim world.

Finally, he met, prayed with and offered support for
his Orthodox confreres: particularly the Ecumenical
Patriarch of Constantinople, Bartholomew I, and the
Armenian Patriarch Mesrob II. He accomplished all
of this with an admirable simplicity and directness
that were heightened by his humble demeanor and
intellectual sincerity. In so doing, he not only won
over many Turks, but furthered one of his chief stated
goals as pope: to advance efforts at greater unity with
the Eastern churches. Considering that the chances for
failure along any one of these fault lines were considerable, and that there had been threats to his physical

safety, we can all offer a collective *Deo gratias* for his achievements and for his safe return.[8]

It seems he is seeking to balance firmness with gentleness.

Theological Truths

This stressing of balance on the part of Benedict the monk and Benedict the pope could also be termed following a path of *via media* or "middle road."

The Church in proclaiming the mysteries of our faith has always pursued that middle course. Consider these examples:

➤ God is awesome, all — everything and beyond us; yet that same God is close to us, within our hearts and compassionate. "O Lord, our God, how awesome is your name though all the earth! You have set your majesty above the heavens!" (Psalm 8:2); "God is present as my helper; the Lord sustains my life" (Psalm 54:6).

➤ Jesus is the Son of God, truly divine, yet Son of Mary, truly human. Christ walked on the water (Matthew 15:22-33); but he also wept over Lazarus (John 11:1-44).

➤ The Church is divinely protected, yet filled with flawed members. "You are Peter, upon this rock I will build my Church, and the gates of the netherworld shall not prevail against it" (Matthew 16:18); "If we say, 'We are without sin,' we deprive ourselves and the truth is not in us. If we acknowledge our sins, he is faithful and just and will forgive our sins and cleanse us from our wrongdoing" (1 John 1: 8-9).

---

[8] *Commonweal*, December 15, 2006, p. 5.

➤ The Eucharist is the Divine Christ before whom we bow in adoration, yet also his Body and Blood which we eat and drink in Holy Communion. "This is my body," "This is my blood" (Mark 14:22-24); "Unless you eat the flesh of the Son of Man and drink his blood, you do not have life within you" (John 6:53).

These truths about the nature of God, Jesus, the Church and the Eucharist are, of course, mysteries. We cannot ever fully grasp them in this world. However, if we overemphasize one aspect of the particular mystery, we come to a distorted understanding of that truth. On the other hand, if we follow the middle of the road, and balance both dimensions of a given mystery, we have a fuller, better and more accurate understanding of that truth.

Pastoral Directives

We have seen in this book how the Church in its basic legal approach and in ritual directives for baptism, marriage and funerals balances fidelity to the message of Christ and flexibility in adjusting to individual circumstances and human weakness.

However, there are many other pastoral directives which reflect that middle road of both fidelity and flexibility. Some may find this combination surprising in certain areas.

➤ The Church teaches that we *must* employ ordinary means of health care for ourselves and others; we also *may* use extraordinary health care procedures for ourselves and others, but are *not obligated* to do so. "Even if death is thought imminent, the ordinary care owed to a sick person cannot be legitimately interrupted" (CCC, Art. 2279). "Discontinuing medical procedures that are burdensome, dangerous, extraordinary, or disproportionate to the expected outcome can be legitimate; it is the refusal of 'over-zealous' treatment" (CCC, Art. 2278).

➤ The Australian Catholic Bishops, commenting on remarks made by Pope John Paul II on two occasions, saw them both as an application of traditional Catholic teaching saying "neither that nutrition and hydration must always be given, nor that they are never to be given, to unresponsive and/or incompetent patients. Rather the Pope affirms the presumption in favor of giving nutrition and hydration to all patients, even by artificial means, which recognizes that in particular cases this presumption gives way to the recognition that the provision of nutrition and hydration would be futile or unduly burdensome."[9]

➤ Pope John Paul II in his final days gave a personal example of the Church's teachings on these end-of-life issues. "In his final two months he was hospitalized twice, had a tracheotomy tube inserted and eventually was assisted in nutrition with a feeding tube."[10] However, during the final forty-eight hours of his life, the Pope was critically and deathly ill, but did not return to the hospital for any extraordinary or heroic measures. Instead he remained in his own home. The "burden of treatment" seemingly outweighed any short-termed prolongation of life. At that point, death was no longer to be resisted, but welcomed as the necessary transition of a Christian life into eternity.[11]

➤ In the past four decades two major liturgical changes were implemented with remarkable ease throughout the United States — Communion in the hand and Communion under

---

[9] Joseph M. Champlin, *Preparing for Eternity* (Notre Dame, IN: Ave Maria Press, 2007), Chapter 2.

[10] *Ibid.*

[11] *Ibid.*

both kinds. Perhaps the reason for this smooth transition was the flexibility or optional nature of the changes. Communicants now were given the choice of receiving the Eucharist in the hand or on the tongue, or of drinking from the cup or declining to do so.

➤ Standing or kneeling for Communion, on the other hand, became an increasingly divisive issue in parishes during the past decade. The diversity of styles disrupted the processional flow to and from the altar, and prompted some to make harsh judgments concerning others, criticizing either their seemingly exaggerated devotion during Holy Communion or their lack of proper respect for the Eucharist. The U.S. Bishops sought to resolve this conflict. Standing for Communion was to be the appropriate method, but no one who knelt was to be denied Communion. In all cases, there was to be a slight reverential bow of the head prior to receiving the consecrated host or the consecrated wine.

➤ The geometrical increase of couples living together before marriage has created a singular challenge for the clergy and pastoral ministers. The reasons for pre-marital cohabitation are many and complex; it is not simply a desire to facilitate sexual relations. But the research is quite definite, stating that cohabitation is neither the morally proper nor even the best way to prepare for marriage. The Church's teaching is quite clear and certain. "The sexual act must take place exclusively within marriage" (CCC, Art. 2390). At the same time, the *Code of Canon Law* states clearly, "All persons who are not prohibited by law can contract marriage" (Canon 1058). Certain canonists would place it in these terms: a person or a couple has a right to marriage; their living together is not in itself an obstacle or impediment to marriage. Some pastors take this approach to cohabiting couples preparing to marry: "While it is not feasible at this time for you to separate, sometime prior to the marriage it would be wise for you to remain sexually inactive, so that the night of the wedding will not simply be the same as the night before the nuptials."

➢ The Church statement that "homosexual acts are intrinsically disordered" makes persons who are gay discouraged, frustrated and even furious (CCC, Art. 2357). Among other reasons given, this teaching is based upon the words noted above that sexual acts are destined exclusively for marriage. Nevertheless, while teaching that homosexual acts are immoral, the *Catechism* states that having homosexual *inclinations* is *not* immoral. The next paragraph speaks to that point and urges a sensitive response to people with homosexual tendencies. It also offers spiritual advice for those struggling with difficulties arising from their condition. "The number of men and women who have deep-seated homosexual tendencies is not negligible. This inclination, which is objectively disordered, constitutes for most of them a trial. They must be accepted with respect, compassion, and sensitivity. Every sign of unjust discrimination in their regard should be avoided. These persons are called to fulfill God's will in their lives and, if they are Christians, to unite to the sacrifice of the Lord's Cross the difficulties they may encounter from their condition" (CCC, Art. 2358).

➢ Clergy and pastoral ministers know from their efforts with youth that masturbation can often be a difficult challenge for adolescents (and for some adults as well). Church teaching in similar fashion states that "masturbation is an intrinsically and gravely disordered action. The deliberate use of the sexual facility, for whatever reason outside of marriage is essentially contrary to its purpose." To balance those succinct, but seemingly severe words, the concluding paragraph of this same section of the *Catechism of the Catholic*

Church calls for compassion: "To form an equitable judgment about the subject's moral responsibility and to guide pastoral action, one must take into account the affective immaturity, force of acquired habit, conditions of anxiety, or other psychological or social factors that lessen or even extenuate moral culpability" (CCC, Art. 2352).

Positive or Pessimistic

Most Rev. Thomas J. Curry is an auxiliary bishop of the Archdiocese of Los Angeles and regional bishop for the Santa Barbara pastoral region. He has written an article entitled "The Best and Worst of Times" seeking an answer to the question why Catholics have remained in the Church during these "terrible" years of the sexual abuse crisis and now, we might add, of current stories about Church fiscal *mis*management.

Bishop Curry finds, in most of the Catholic commentaries he has read, a pessimism about the Church, a polarization among its members and even a ferocity about the ills of the Church which equals that of "the most ardent anti-Catholics."

During pastoral visits over four years in his area he has not discovered that pessimism, polarization or negative ferocity. Instead he has experienced "optimism, commitment and a widespread willingness to face the challenges confronting the Church." He has witnessed "the fidelity, courage and stubbornness of the American Catholic people." He has observed "a profound sense of attachment to the Church they have created since the council."

Those who seem preoccupied with pessimism and polarization seek a solution in two ways. He writes: "The right would attempt to return the Church to an idealized past" (not so ideal as we mentioned earlier in connection with the annulment process); "the left would assimilate the Church into the dominant ethos."

When Bishop Curry asks congregations why they have stayed and not left during these "worst of times," their responses seem to reflect the words of St. Paul: "We hold this treasure in earthen vessels, that the surpassing power may be of God and not from us" (2 Corinthians 4:7).

In effect those congregations view these dark incidents in the Church as the weakness of some (a small minority at that), not a disease permeating the entire body. They acknowledge sin, but believe more in the greater power of grace. They are confident that God will bring light and goodness out of darkness and evil.[12]

In certain ways the people of that California region mirror the faith of the late and great historian Father John Tracy Ellis. Speaking to the Boston clergy gathered for a celebration of priest jubilarians (long before the sexual crisis surfaced there), he proclaimed that next to his belief in Jesus' words about being always present in the Church, his greatest source of hope was his knowledge of the history of the Church.

Another historian more than a century earlier, made his famous remark that if any organization or society had known the corruption from within or persecution from without which the Church has experienced, it would have long ago perished.

It is, then a Church, sinful and constantly in need of reform or repentance, but a Church filled always with the presence and protection of Christ.

The Church thus survives and even flourishes throughout dark moments of purification.

---

[12] Most Rev. Thomas J. Curry, "The Best and Worst of Times," *America*, November 20, 2006, pp. 20-23.

A Challenge and a Comfort

Father Robert Nugent, S.D.S., writing in *Church* magazine, urges clergy today to share an evening meal several nights a week. The purpose of his recommendation:

Sharing an evening meal several nights a week creates a fraternal bond. Given the variety of personalities, ages, ecclesiologies, theologies, pastoral styles, and preferences among priests, we must learn to listen to and respect one another's views. Instead of complaining about the "younger and more conservative John Paul priests" or the "older, liberal Vatican II priests," all of us have to work in the vineyard together.[13]

I hope that this book may achieve his goal of bringing priests of different perspectives together, working in closer harmony for a common cause.

However, my intended audience is much wider, embracing not only priests, but all clergy and the many persons involved in various aspects of pastoral ministry today.

Those on both sides of the ideological divide should find in these pages a challenge and a comfort.

For those who hold strong convictions about being faithful to Christ's teachings, strictly adhering to the Church's directives, and raising the bar for all Catholics, this book should be a comfort. It will reassure those individuals that their effort to stretch people by urging them on to better lives, a more faithful following of Jesus' message and an awareness of the negatives in our contemporary culture, fits the officially firm and faithful dimension throughout this volume.

---

[13] Robert Nugent, S.D.S., "The Pope and the Parakeet: What Ever Happened to Rectory Meals? (The Case for Common Meals)," *Church*, Fall 2006, pp. 20-23.

At the same time, the officially flexible dimension may challenge them to be more kind, gentle and bending in practical dealings with their people.

Those who by temperament and ideology tend to be kind, gentle and bending in their dealings with people should find that the officially flexible aspects likewise provide a comfort, reassuring them that their own easily adjustable pastoral paths most often can find support in Church directives.

At the same time, they will no doubt be challenged by the officially faithful dimension in this book, asking themselves if in their desire to please or adjust, they may have neglected or not thoroughly enough communicated what are the Church's higher expectations for its people.

I would like to conclude this book by placing it under the protection of Mary, the Mother of the Church.

St. Germanus in his homily on the Presentation of the Mother of God, celebrated commonly on November 21, addresses her in Eastern fashion with eloquent phrases such as "Hail, holy throne of God, divine sanctuary, house of glory...." Then he pleads: "By your most acceptable prayers, strong with authority of motherhood, to our Lord and God... steer the ship of the Church and bring it to a quiet harbor."[14]

May Mary, the Mother of the Church, steer clergy and pastoral ministers during this best of times and worst of times, bringing all of us to a quiet harbor.

---

[14] Leonard Foley, O.F.M. and Pat McCloskey, O.F.M., *Saint of the Day, op. cit.*, pp. 299-300.

AFTERWORD AND ACKNOWLEDGMENTS

When *The Marginal Catholic* first appeared about two decades ago, *U.S. Catholic* invited me to Chicago for a discussion about the concepts in that book.

During the course of a several hour exchange with their editorial staff, one person asked me: "Isn't the Church legalistic?"

I replied: "The official Church isn't legalistic, but some Church leaders are."

Noble motives and good intentions prompted at that time what might be termed certain legalistic approaches in parishes. The clergy and pastoral ministers were concerned that those seeking especially marriage and baptism possessed sufficient faith and that the sacraments would work or bear fruit.

For example, *Time* magazine featured an illustrated story about a bishop from the Southwest announcing a change in marriage preparation procedures. Because of the rapid increase in divorces, he said, they were seeking to stem that tide by introducing a series of somewhat restrictive measures. These included a mandatory waiting period, extensive required classes and specialized psychological tests. These, valuable in themselves, were nevertheless susceptible to an overly rigid application.

Some diocesan family life offices subsequently developed similar procedures. One, in particular, required three different decisions to be made before an engaged couple were allowed to reserve the church for their nuptials.

The official Church, in the person of Pope John Paul II and his 1981 document, *The Christian Family in the Modern World*, which we cited in Chapter 8, had the effect of curbing that trend. Describing the only disposition essential for a couple seeking marriage in the Church and warning against further external criteria for determining their readiness, the Holy Father thus discouraged procedures like the multiple decision process of that diocese we mentioned.

I sensed following publication of this papal document, a softening of approach on both the diocesan and parish levels.

Another example: The insistence upon parents attending Mass and registering in the parish as requisites for baptism was not uncommon throughout the United States.

Once again, the official Church, through several Vatican offices, intervened. They gently suggested to bishops of a certain region, making their *ad limina* visit to Rome, that in the United States there was a tendency to impose too restrictive conditions upon baptism. That message soon spread throughout the nation.

As with marriage, I detected, following those exchanges, a gradual softening of approach, also on both the diocesan and parish levels.

Today, those noble concerns about faith and fruitfulness continue. However, a new attitude appears to have crept into pastoral ministry. There is, among some, a rigidity, an emphasis on the letter instead of upon the spirit of the law, a strict application of rules with no exceptions or adaptations.

A clergyman or pastoral minister, as one illustration, prohibited underage sponsors for baptism. Either that individual did not know the explicit exception which the *Code of Canon Law* allowed or interpreted too severely the "just cause" required.

Parishes, for a second illustration, established rather strict local rules governing the celebration of the sacraments. While they could be considered appropriate, the clergy were unbending in their application, never entertaining the possibility of exceptions in particular circumstances. Insisting upon preparation classes prior to baptism surely is a praiseworthy directive. However, when this is the second or third child and parish leaders demand attendance at the exactly identical session which both parents experienced even at great inconvenience for infant number one, such rigid insistence seems inappropriate.

With an overly determined goal of being firm and faithful, this attitude minimizes or neglects the Church's official flexibility and gentleness.

Seeking a Balance

To maintain a balance between fidelity and flexibility, between firmness and gentleness, as this book tries to accomplish, was and is a delicate and challenging task. I needed assistance with the writing and received wonderful help from many persons. To them I am deeply grateful.

All agreed that the book was needed and gave it their encouragement. Some offered detailed suggestions. That input prompted me to make over 1,000 corrections in the second draft — often only a word or phrase change, but also several substantive additions or alterations. For the third draft, there were a further 100 revisions.

Recommendations from those dozen readers made this an improved and better manuscript.

My thanks to:

◆ Father Edmund C. Lane, S.S.P. of Alba House accepted the manuscript for publication and, as he and his team did with the Revised and Updated Edition of *The Marginal Catholic,* worked hard to produce a very attractive book.

◆ Ms. Patricia Livingston of Tampa, Florida not only endorsed the idea, but gave it a very helpful specific direction in the beginning stages as well as offering many detailed comments after reading the first draft. She, in addition, recommended the Resource Section at the end of this book.

◆ Father John Eudes Bamberger, O.C.S.O., the retired Abbot for the Abbey of the Genesee in Piffard, New York, likewise saw a need for this book and suggested that the manuscript possess a certain tone or thrust.

◆ Father Kevin McKenna, whose pastoral experience, canonical expertise and positive comments contributed in a major way during the writing of this book.

◆ Bishop Thomas Costello, a friend for a half-century and a very skilled editor, through his many insightful comments made this a more fluid text and insured that the contents were faithful to Catholic teaching.

◆ Father Don Krebs, a retired parish priest who nevertheless serves as a faculty member in Milwaukee at the Hales Corners Sacred Heart Seminary for second career men studying to be priests, sees a great need for this book in their preparation of future clergy for pastoral work. He also provided a dozen specific suggestions to improve the text.

◆ Sister Maureen D'Onofrio, C.S.J., pastoral associate at the Syracuse Cathedral of the Immaculate Conception, offered spontaneous and enthusiastic encouragement at a critical point during the writing process.

◆ Mrs. Ann Tyndall, my administrative assistant during the past two years, who with great skill and patience completed the complex process of converting my hand written text into a computerized document and then making the over 1,100 corrections in the several drafts.

◆ The following, in various ways, made important contributions to this book: Rosemary Carr, William Cosgrove, Michael Donovan, James Drew, Dennis Hayes, Thomas Hobbes, Ronald Jameson, David and Nancy Kreis, Ron Lewinski, John Roark, Michael Ryan, Kathleen Slate, Barbara Smith and Wilbur Votraw.

RESOURCES

An early reader of my manuscript suggested a list of resources which might prove helpful with the implementation of ideas in this book.

The texts below are by no means an exhaustive list, merely those publications I found helpful in my over 50 years of pastoral ministry. I offer these references with some reluctance since many come from my pen. Those were written, however, in response to needs I experienced in parish life.

Reference Texts

Vatican Council II: The Conciliar and Post Conciliar Documents (Costello). A reading, or more probably a re-reading of the *Constitution on the Sacred Liturgy* will place the past and present specific liturgical changes in proper perspective.

Catechism of the Catholic Church (Doubleday): This most recent compendium of official Catholic teaching is cited frequently in *Firm, But Kind and Gentle*.

The *ritual books for baptism, marriage and funerals*. The Introductions in each of these texts contain rich theological and pastoral information.

The Marginal Catholic: Challenge Don't Crush. Published originally in 1989 (Ave Maria Press) and then in a Revised and Updated Edition with reference to the *Catechism of the Catholic Church* in 2001 (Alba House). *Firm, But Kind*

and Gentle: A Practical Handbook for Pastoral Ministry is a
sequel to *The Marginal Catholic*. Much, but not all of the
material in that earlier book has made its way, although in
different fashion, into the current text. Moreover, *Firm,
But Kind and Gentle* addresses many new concerns and
adds numerous further suggestions for serving God's
people today in an effective manner.

Pastoral Aids

What It Means To Be Catholic (St. Anthony Messenger Press).
A colorful, 81/2" x 11", beautifully illustrated 64 page
booklet, published originally in 1987 and in a stunning,
updated version in 2007, emphasizes how major Catholic
teachings and practices respond to the yearnings and needs
of people today. It has been used frequently on the parish
level for Inquiry Sessions, pre-Evangelization series, the
RCIA, Confirmation processes and for individuals not
Catholic, who seek to marry a Catholic in the Church.

A User-Friendly Parish (Twenty-Third Publications). This paperback contains a wealth of practical suggestions on how to
develop a truly "welcoming parish."

Your Baby's Baptism (Liquori). A well-illustrated 16 page 8 1/4" x
11 5/8" publication is an excellent booklet and very popular with parents as they approach their parish to arrange a
baptism. Available in English and Spanish.

"An Understanding and Agreement for a Sponsor or Godparent
at Baptism and Confirmation." This single page form,
printed front and back, has been developed and used suc-
cessfully in three quite different parishes over a 25 year
span. It eliminates much of the tension which arises over
the question of sponsors or godparents. A sample appears
at the end of this section and could easily be adapted for
any parish.

"An Invitation." A sample of this invitation to the baptism is also reproduced at the end of this section and could easily be revised for local use. Explaining and distributing a half-dozen of these to the parents invariably prompts immediate surprise and approving smiles from them.

Together for Life (Ave Maria Press). The Regular (Marriage with Mass) and Special (Marriage Outside Mass), both in English and Spanish, have been used by a majority of couples married by a Catholic priest for more than thirty years.

From the Heart (Ave Maria Press). A small booklet which describes the process of "Hopes and Expectations" for the marriage celebration and includes ten samples from actual weddings. Chapter 8 of *Firm, But Kind and Gentle* begins with an example of such "Hopes and Expectations."

Should We Marry? (Ave Maria Press). This paperback provides insights for the questions "Is This the Person for Me?" and "Should We Live Together First?" The latter offers substantial material about cohabitation.

"10 Questions About Annulment" (Catholic Update). A relatively inexpensive four page, 8 1/2" x 11" publication in the familiar *Catholic Update* format, it can be helpful as a handout for any person seeking an annulment or concerned about one.

Meeting the Merciful Christ: How to Go to Confession (St. Anthony Messenger Press). This pamphlet explains the why and how of Penance or Reconciliation and may be given to the couple a few months before the marriage, ideally in connection with completing the prenuptial inquiry questionnaire.

A Thoughtful Word, A Healing Touch (Twenty-Third Publications). Subtitled "A Guide for Visiting the Sick," the pamphlet is particularly useful for families gathered around critically ill members.

Through Death to Life (Ave Maria Press). The booklet has become increasingly popular for the clergy, pastoral ministers, and bereavement committees as they work with families preparing to celebrate the Funeral Mass.

Death and Life (Ave Maria Press). A 30 minute VHS video which
explains the Funeral Mass and ways members of the family can participate in the preparation and celebration of
it. When pastoral ministers are able to visit the home of
the surviving family soon after the death occurs and leave
the video with them, the bereaved frequently find viewing *Death and Life* is both inspirational and informative,
facilitating the use of *Through Death to Life.*

The Rite of Marriage and *The Funeral Mass and Rite of Committal
Ritual Cards* (Ave Maria Press). These ritual cards and
companion binders make it possible for the presiding
clergy easily and quickly to arrange cards with the prayers,
readings and blessings selected by the couple or family,
then insert them in an appropriate and attractive binder
for use during the actual celebration.

Preparing for Eternity: A Catholic Handbook for End of Life Concerns
(Ave Maria Press). Its ten chapters begin with "Making
a Will" and "Cremation," then conclude with "A Com-
forting Farewell," "Eternity," and "Those Left Behind."

An Understanding and Agreement for a Sponsor or Godparent at Baptism or Confirmation

Role of Sponsor or Godparent

It is an ancient custom of the Church that at the baptism of infants, godparents be present to represent the expanded spiritual family of the child being baptized and the role of the Church as a mother. Later, godparents help the parents so that children will profess the faith chosen for them and live up to it. Each baptized child may have either a godfather or godmother or both a godmother and a godfather.

Requirements for a Sponsor or Godparent

1. The godparent should be *mature enough* to understand, accept and carry out the duties of a godparent. That person normally should be at least 16 years of age, but exceptions are possible.
2. The godparent ordinarily must *have received* the *three initiation sacraments* — baptism, confirmation and Eucharist.
3. The godparent should be *living an exemplary life* consistent with the faith and the responsibilities of a godparent through attendance at Church and following the teaching of Christ's Church.
4. The godparent must be a *member of the Catholic Church.* However, a baptized and believing Christian not belonging to the Catholic Church may act as a Christian witness as long as there is also a Catholic godparent.

Functions of a Godparent

1. Stand on either side of parents since the mother or father usually holds the infant.
2. Respond "We are" to this question at the initial part or reception rite: "Are you ready to help the parents of this child in their duty as Christian parents?"
3. Trace a sign of the cross on the child's forehead at the conclusion of the reception rite.
4. Listen to this admonition at the Renunciation of Sin and Profession of Faith:

   "Dear Parents and Godparents: You have come here to present this child for baptism. By water and the Holy Spirit he (she) is to receive the gift of new life from God, who is love.

   On your part, you must make it your constant care to bring her (him) up in the practice of the faith. See that the divine life which God gives her (him) is kept safe from the poison of sin, to grow always stronger in her (his) heart.

If your faith makes you ready to accept this responsibility, renew now the vows of your own baptism. Reject sin; profess your faith in Christ Jesus. This is the faith of the Church. This is the faith in which this child is about to be baptized.

5. Respond "I do" to these questions:

"Do you reject sin, so as to live in the freedom of God's children?"

"Do you reject the glamour of evil, and refuse to be mastered by sin?"

"Do you reject Satan, father of sin and prince of darkness?"

"Do you believe in God, the Father almighty, creator of heaven and earth?"

"Do you believe in Jesus Christ, his only Son our Lord, who was born of the Virgin Mary, was crucified, died, and was buried, rose from the dead, and is now seated at the right hand of the Father?"

"Do you believe in the Holy Spirit, the Holy Catholic Church, the communion of saints, the forgiveness of sins, the resurrection of the body, and life everlasting?"

6. Respond "Amen" to and/or repeat this summary of faith: "This is our faith. This is the faith of the Church. We are proud to profess it, in Christ Jesus our Lord."

7. Touch the child during the actual pouring of water.

8. Light the baptismal candle from the Easter candle and present it to the father.

9. Join in the Our Father and the other responses during the baptismal rite.

Understanding and Agreement

I understand my role, the requirements and my function as a godparent or sponsor for:

Child's name

and
I accept these responsibilities

Godparent's signature

Please mail this completed form to the rectory or drop it in the collection at least one week beforehand.

An Invitation

Our Child

_____

will be welcomed into
the Catholic Church
through the waters of Baptism

on _____

at _____ *o'clock*

Our Lady of Good Counsel
6421 Newport Road
Warners, New York

We cordially invite you
to participate in this celebration with us.

_____

ST PAULS

This book was produced by ST PAULS/Alba House, the Society of St. Paul, an international religious congregation of priests and brothers dedicated to serving the Church through the communications media.

For information regarding this and associated ministries of the Pauline Family of Congregations, write to the Vocation Director, Society of St. Paul, 2187 Victory Blvd., Staten Island, New York 10314-6603. Phone (718) 982-5709; or E-mail: vocation@stpauls.us or check our internet site, www.vocationoffice.org